THE SOUL OF A HORSE
BLOGGED

THE JOURNEY CONTINUES

THE SOUL OF A HORSE
BLOGGED

THE JOURNEY CONTINUES

LIVE THE MOMENTS

Inspiring New Stories - Compelling New Discoveries

JOE CAMP

14 HANDS PRESS

Also by Joe Camp

The Soul of a Horse
Life Lessons from the Herd

Who Needs Hollywood
The Amazing Story of a Small Time Filmmaker
Who Writes the Screenplay, Raises the Production Budget,
Directs, and Distributes the #3 Movie of the Year

Born To Be Wild
The Soul of a Mustang
Riding the Winds of Change

For more: www.14handspress.com

Copyright © 2010 by Joe Camp

All rights reserved.

Published in the United States by 14 Hands Press,

an imprint of Camp Horse Camp, LLC

www.14handspress.com

Library of Congress Control Number: 2010910522

Library of Congress subject headings

Camp, Joe

The Soul of a Horse BLOG / by Joe Camp

Horses

Human-animal relationships

Horses-health

Horsemanship

The Soul of a Horse: Life Lessons from the Herd

ISBN 978-1-930681-04-0

First Edition

I want to thank each of you who caused our publication year to be so incredibly special by helping to push *The Soul of a Horse* into seven printings and make it an official best seller. We are indebted to you all and appreciate you very much. This expanded blog, this continuation of that journey which began with *The Soul of a Horse,* is for you. And for every horse on the planet.

— Joe Camp

CONTENTS

THE SOUL OF A HORSE
BLOGGED
THE JOURNEY CONTINUES

INTRODUCTION

So how did it happen? One day we were complete novices, without a horse or a clue. The next day we had three horses. And a short year-and-a-half later I was writing a book about this new journey that would wind up changing the lives of horses (and people) all across the planet.

My head is still spinning.

I look back in awe, wondering how I had the gall to even think about writing such a book, never mind actually doing it. Almost always books like *The Soul of a Horse* are written by folks with decades of experience on the subject. I *did* have decades of experience trying to lure you into the heart and soul of a floppy-eared dog, but now I was blatantly trying to lure you into the heart and soul of a horse. Because when I stumbled into the heart and soul of my very special Cash I discovered that something was very wrong with the way we think about horses.

If the last Benji movie, *Benji Off the Leash,* had been a big success, this journey would not have happened and *The Soul of a Horse* would've never been written. The movie was unable to compete as an independent film against the huge promotional dollars being spent by the Hollywood studios these days. That experience left a huge, gaping hole in my life. I was convinced that *Benji Off the*

Leash was going to raise the bar for family films. Be an example that would show Hollywood the error of its ways. It had a strong story that set a good example, without the use of four-letter words, sexual innuendos, or violence. I was certain that God was using *Benji Off the Leash* to prove once and for all that good stories do not need to lower the bar to entertain. It was clear, at least to me, that God had been involved in the movie from the beginning, that He wanted it to be made. The money was raised in record time. We were forced to accept Utah as a production location, against our wishes, but once we were there, many of the usual production problems miraculously vanished. And we found Tony DiLorenzo, a young composer searching for his first movie. He wrote an amazing score that we could never have afforded with a seasoned composer, and I believe Tony will become one of the finest film composers in the business.

Yet with all of that, the film did not do well.

Growth always seems to rise out of adversity.

I, of course, didn't know it when it was happening, but God was telling me it was time to move on. Another need. Another place to make a difference.

If the movie had been even marginally successful, He knew I'd be off working on another one.

But I wasn't to go there.

It was decided that I would turn to horses. And God recruited Kathleen to do the dirty work, to lead me unwittingly down this path. Until, quite unexpectedly, an amazing journey of discovery spread out before me.

A new passion was born.

And for that I thank God.

And Kathleen, His accomplice.

So if in any way our journey has helped you or your horses, thank those two. It's all their fault.

Of course when the book was published we didn't stop learning and when the responses started pouring in I was moved to keep
writing about our continuing journey. Many of you seemed to identify with our stumbling around in search of better, more appropriate ways to keep and care for our horses. Our newsletter and blog
were ultimately merged into a single content that more or less began with the next major step in our journey. The adoption of an
untouched pregnant mustang from the Bureau of Land Management.

Putting the blog into book form was your idea. Or the idea of
some of you. Those who kept saying you would rather have a book
on your nightstand than a computer. So for those who feel that
way, here it is. Twenty-three months of blog posts. Expanded because unfortunately I couldn't leave any of it alone. You know how
it is with hindsight. Distance from the subject. Things are so much
clearer now than they were then. Or so it seems. And we've added
more photos.

But please understand this is not the promised follow-up, the
sequel if you will, to *The Soul of a Horse*. The next *real* book, *Born
To Be Wild*, will be written as a book, not a journal. It will contain
the lessons *behind* the lessons we've been learning from the horses,
both domestic and wild, and the continuing story of the wild herd
so many of you seemed to love. And it will explore the illegal acts
committed by the Bureau of Land Management against that herd,
and all of our horses in the wild.

But this book is a blog. A skeleton. The high points of our
continuing journey, the tip of the iceberg so to speak. More or less
the *Sparknotes* version of that next book (the first three chapters of
which are included at the end of this journal by the way). If you
haven't read the blog, I hope you will enjoy this and absorb benefit
from these lessons taught by the horses. If you have followed the
blog or newsletter I hope these expanded posts, all together in one

volume, will stir a new insight perhaps missed in a quick earlier reading; be a nudge toward putting relationship first with your horses. And doing whatever it takes to give them better health, happiness, and longer lives. For that is our only objective.

- Joe Camp

PART ONE

BRINGING UP BABY

1

A PREGNANT MUSTANG FOR CHRISTMAS

On the evening of December 20th, 2008, we arrived home with my Christmas gift from Kathleen, an untouched pregnant Mustang adopted from the BLM in Reno, a six-year-old buckskin lady who chose us – well, chose Kathleen. I had missed her completely in our survey of the 150 or so mares in the five-and-over pasture at the BLM facility the week before.

Just imagine being the very first person ever to be touched by a wild Mustang, and being the first person to touch her foal. Shivers skitter up my spine every time I think about it. Two horses who will begin their journey with humans... with us.

Adoptions Manager John Parsons had sent dozens of photos of several possibilities. We flew up from San Diego on December 10th to make our selection and were driven around and around through the large herd, first isolating John's photos, then trying to check out the other 145 or so. Around and around we'd go.

The black one was very pregnant but seemed a bit sluggish and not very curious. One of the grays was very dominant. Dr. Matt had warned against that. Another gray was being moved around by everyone in sight. And so far only one seemed really curious about us but she was almost certainly not pregnant. It was important that our choice be pregnant because the birth of her foal would be the foreword to my next book. John kept driving.

"Wait, can you back up a bit?"

It was Kathleen speaking.

"Now forward. Whoa."

The shutter on her camera clicked. I turned to see where it was pointing.

"What about her?" she was asking John.

"The buckskin?" he asked.

"Yes. She keeps looking at us."

"She doesn't seem too dominant, but not wimpy. Alert. Very curious. Kind eyes. I like her. I like her a lot."

And Kathleen wondered why I had insisted that she come along.

After another thirty minutes of driving around, always coming back to Kathleen's buckskin, John and I agreed with her and we headed to the office to fill out the paperwork, me wondering why this mare hadn't been in the library of photos they had sent to us. But I didn't ask. We were off to the airport three hours earlier than expected. The plan was that we'd drive up three days later to pick her up. I couldn't wait. My portable GPS said the drive from Valley Center would be between ten and eleven hours, much of it through the mountains with elevations up to 8100 feet. What none of us remembered to do when the plan was made was to check the weather. Weather systems seemed to be running rampant off the west coast, rolling in every few days. Our travel plans were scuttled by five days of snow, wind and rain. I studied the 10-day forecast at weather.com plus everything the California Highway Patrol site had to say. John at the BLM advised that from now through February or March things would only get worse. There appeared to be a 2-day window between storms the following Friday and Saturday (December 19-20) if the highways at upper elevations were clear. I told John this was our target and I began to monitor the CHP site several times a day.

The afternoon before we were to leave home the CHP still had two sections of highway closed due to snow from the last storm, but Friday morning they were both clear. One section well to the north was still showing wind warnings, but the forecast from weather.com was 15mph by afternoon, so off we went, sandwiched between two bad weather systems, creating a serious need to have everything work right. Never the best strategy. This would be the longest trip I'd ever driven with a horse trailer and as we started out I was thankful that trucks don't read nervousness like horses do.

The trip, mercifully, was on time and relatively uneventful. CHP was still predicting high winds over a twenty mile stretch of highway maybe 100 miles out of Reno but weather.com said no, so we bit our lips and ignored the brightly flashing wind-warning signs and kept going. Weather.com was right.

I had found a hotel with a big open parking lot that could take a horse trailer, a casino unfortunately right in the middle of downtown. We locked up the truck and trailer and ice-skated across the street to a very mediocre dinner but a very warm bed. The next morning we were at it early. The temperature was a frigid 15 degrees, a condition I had never experienced with a diesel truck. At first it wouldn't start at all, which scared me to death. Finally it turned over, but the accelerator wasn't working, had no effect at all. And an engine warning light was on… on a Saturday morning! And snow was due in Reno Saturday night.

I let the engine run for almost thirty minutes before the water temperature gauge finally reached into its working range. But the engine light was still on. While the engine was still warming up I unlocked all the trailer doors. Well, not all the trailer doors because the key would not turn at all in the lock of the tack room where all the feed and buckets were for the trip home. Kathleen returned to the hotel and called several 24-hours locksmiths, none of whom were answering their phones. She left a cell number. Once the water temperature gauge was in operating range everything seemed to be operating properly so I decided we should drive on out to the BLM, 15 miles north of town. Maybe the engine light would go out as the engine continued to warm up.

It didn't.

On the way out, Kathleen called both of Reno's Dodge dealers. Again, no answers. Just great, I was thinking. We simply could not take off through the mountains with an unhandled pregnant Mustang and an engine warning light on.

When we arrived at the BLM John Parsons and several bright-eyed, eager volunteers were happily awaiting the loading of another Mustang saved.

"Welcome," John said. "Let's get to it."

"Sorry John," I said meekly, "We have a couple of problems we need to deal with before we can load up." I explained the problems. John felt that he could find us a diesel mechanic who could look at the problem… and maybe WD40 would take care of the lock. His diesel mechanic was not answering the phone at 7:30 am so he headed out to attack the lock on the trailer tack room. As he strolled past the truck – I've never been able to "stroll" at 15 degrees – he asked casually, "Are you sure your gas cap is screwed down good and tight? Sometimes a loose cap can cause the engine light to come on."

Kathleen whipped open the flap and turned the cap. "Nope," she said. "It was not screwed down to the click."

I raced to the truck cab and turned the key. The engine light was gone. I felt like a ton of bricks had been lifted off my heart.

John then tried WD40 on the lock, but that yielded nothing. He studied it for a moment, and said, "Let me try something." Soon he returned with a small blow torch. He ignited it and aimed it right at the culprit lock. Thirty seconds later we were inside the tack room. I asked him if he could ride back to Valley Center with us. "What's the temperature down there," he grinned.

The loading went very smoothly. The BLM's elaborate system of stalls and aisles with closing and opening doors made it very simple. I walked down to look in on her before they started. She was standing all alone in a very large stall. She turned and looked at me with that quizzical cock of a head that is often offered up by my Cash. I couldn't help but smile.

"Hello Miss Noelle," I said.

Noelle would be her name. She was, after all, Kathleen's Christmas gift to me.

"We're off on an adventure, you and I," I said to her. "A new journey for both of us. I will love you. And I believe you will love me." I walked back down the long aisle to the squeeze chute positioned just before the trailer. One of the volunteers opened a gate to let me out of the maze and I grabbed my camera out of the truck and climbed onto the platform over the squeeze chute. I cannot fathom why we had not brought the video camera but we hadn't so Kathleen was going to shoot video with her tiny digital still camera and I'd shoot stills with the Nikon.

I'm not sure why this moment had such an impact on me but I shivered a bit as I waited for her to appear, and not from the cold.

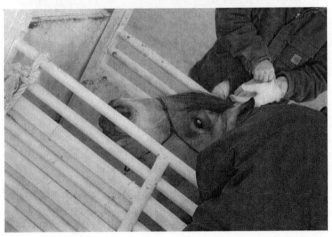

All went perfectly. She trotted down the hallway system, urged on quietly by John and the volunteers. Doors shut behind her every 20 to 30 feet until she was in the squeeze chute where John tied on a rope halter I had given him. Just in case.

They opened the squeeze chute and she trotted straight into the trailer without urging.

I had wanted to be on the road by 8:30, and even with all the issues, we were. We said our thank you's and goodbyes and left them three copies of *The Soul of a Horse*. Then we were off. The trip home was thankfully uneventful. The CHP was still predicting high winds in the same area as before but weather.com said light and variable. Once again, weather.com was right. All was going well.

Until we got home.

Noelle would not leave the trailer.

I had prepared a plan to set up stall panels so she could come out, turn right, and trot straightaway into her new paddock. The tires had to be chocked because the driveway is very steep where we would be unloading. Once set, we swung open the back door and waited. She didn't move. She wasn't at all interested in leaving the trailer. It hadn't occurred to me that it might bother her to turn around and face down hill in order to step out. Especially with wobbly legs from the long ride home.

At the BLM the folks walking behind her had shaken long sticks with plastic bags tied to one end to keep her moving in the right direction.

"We have one in the tack room," Kathleen urged.

I shook my head, not wanting her to associate me with those who had extracted her from her home in the wild.

"She *has* to come out," Kathleen said. "We're all very tired."

"I think it's the downhill thing. If the door were *up* the hill instead of down I think she'd come out."

"I think you're too tired to think straight," Kathleen said.

She was right. I went to an enormous amount of trouble to drive up to the house, turn the trailer around, drive it back down the hill to the paddock, re-chock the tires and rebuild the chute to the paddock.

And she still wouldn't come out.

"Here," Kathleen said and handed me the stick with a plastic bag attached. "Use it."

Noelle backed right out of the trailer and trotted into the paddock. And I'm convinced she would have done exactly the same thing the first time had I used the stick. It was all about what she knew.

And what I didn't.

Or what I had forgotten.

It wasn't the last time I would forget that simplicity is the essence of good communication. With a horse, or with anyone.

But at least Noelle was home.

We had done it, and it felt good. Kathleen and I leaned on the fence and just gazed at her for quite some time. We had a beautiful mustang, fresh from the wild. And she would never have to worry about an unbelievable death threat from our very own federal government. I wanted to go into the paddock and give her a big hug. Like I would Cash. Or Mariah.

"She isn't Cash or Mariah," Kathleen said.

Of course we both knew that was true. But neither of us had any idea how true, nor where all this was leading us.

As I write this, today is Day 15, the two-week anniversary of Noelle's arrival. She has yet to touch me, but she is eating hay out of my hand, she trots up to the fence whenever I or Kathleen show up, she's very comfortable chomping away as little as three or four feet from us when we're sitting in the pasture with her, but that's her bubble of safety.

And whereas that bubble is getting smaller every day, at the moment that's about as close as her comfort level will allow. I believe it's an unconscious thing. Horses are hardwired to react first and ask questions later, to be freaky about everything, and I believe in my heart that she simply cannot help herself. That's as close as she can get at the moment without reacting. I can see her wanting to be closer, but after reaching, trying, you can see it in her eyes. I just can't. I can't help it. It's just too much. And I must wait. After all, she has never seen a human who wasn't trying to round her up and take her away from her family, out of the wild, or squeeze her into a chute to stick her with needles. Or chase her from one place to another.

Patience is not my strong suit. Our horses have all taught me to do better in that department. But I'm going to have to do even better with Noelle. She has already taught me that, much to my embarrassment.

I hope you'll stick with our gentling of this sweet mare and the birth of her foal. Two fewer wild mustangs living under government threat and control.

2

DAY 46
NOELLE TOUCHES

This morning Kathleen said to me, "Do you realize that you're always saying, 'I wonder when I'm going to be able to do this or do that with Noelle.' Just a few days ago you were saying you couldn't wait until you could scratch her on the neck. Seriously, just a few days! And here you are scratching her neck, her chest, her leg, her ear, her face and are you satisfied, even just a little bit? Have you taken a moment to just sigh happily and say gee this is only Day 46 and look how well we're doing?"

"Well, I thought it," I said. "I think I thought it."

"I don't believe it. You only thought: *I wonder when I'll be able to do it all on her left side... or when will I be brushing her tail and trimming her feet for goodness sake.*"

"Gotta think ahead," says I.

She tossed a pleading look Heavenward and said, "It's not working. That business about teaching him patience, it's not working."

Fortunately, she said it with a smile. But she does have a point. As I finally stepped up to the task of writing this post I actually had to go back and read some of the earlier notes just to see where we were when, and I was amazed. Only nine days ago I couldn't even touch her on her jaw. Thirty days ago she wouldn't even get close to me. When she arrived, she had never been touched by anyone... willingly. She's leaping thresholds like an Olympic champion.

On Day 15 she and Benji actually "joined-up" completely on their own. They sniffed noses and touched each other. Unfortunately we didn't have a camera in the paddock at the time, and the funny thing is that Benji won't get within 20 feet of our other horses, even Cash.

On Day 16, she crept up behind me and actually took a bite from a bowl only three feet away.

I had been sitting quietly in one place for at least 15 or 20 minutes. A couple of times she had approached but Kathleen stopped her in her tracks by raising the camera to shoot. Finally patience paid off (and, yes, it seems weird for me to be saying that about me). She reached out and took a bite, and didn't even react to multiple shutter clicks. At last. Noelle, the bowl, and me, all within a three-foot circle.

Three days later, Kathleen captured my favorite Noelle video with her little point-and shoot camera. I was sitting on a rock holding the bowl, just being silent, and still. Waiting. For most of the time it seemed to me that nothing whatsoever was happening and I was wondering why Kathleen continued to shoot, but when I saw the video I was astounded at how much you could see going on in Noelle's eyes as she tried to come to the bowl again and again but just couldn't. She'd turn away, or back away, over and over before she finally reached.... stretched... and took a nibble. Then another... and another... until the bowl was clean.

It's a great lesson in the rewards of patience. And somehow just knowing that such results actually do materialize helps me with my genetic disposition to always hurry up. Doesn't get rid of it by any means but it does motivate me to sit on it for a while and wait for the good stuff. Do take a look at the video. If you can make it through to the end you'll never forget it. It's in the right hand column on *The Soul of a Horse* website or blog. Look for Video - Day 18.

This was apparently a major threshold, patience well rewarded, as the breakthroughs began to come one right after another over the next few days. Even Benji got into the act.

On Day 20 she first took hay from my hand. On Day 25 she first allowed a few rubs on her cheek.

On Day 26, I was sitting on the ground in the paddock with my back to Noelle, talking to Dani, our trimmer. Noelle was down the hill and to my rear. I heard her coming up but did not look around.

Just kept talking. Dani interrupted me and said "Oh, you should've seen that. Something freaked her down by the fence and she came straight to you. She considers you her safe place." She stopped about five feet behind me and just stood there, head down, for quite a while. After a bit, she exhaled a couple of times and wandered back to whatever she was doing. This was very cool.

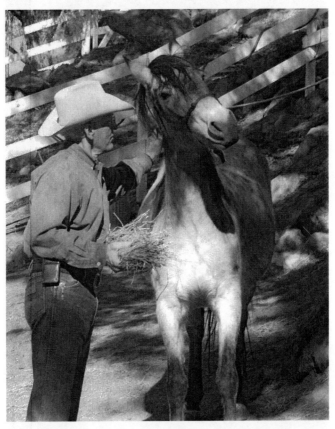

I continue to see in her eyes that she wants more than she can give right now. When no food is offered, if I reach out slowly to touch her cheek, she'll sometimes turn, even slower, just an inch or two... as if she's saying: I must turn away but I don't want to really so I'll just move slower than you so your hand will catch up. But I don't catch up. I stop where her head was, and smile, and withdraw.

When her nose is on the ground, nibbling dregs, I go down with my face and get my nose within inches of hers. She continues to nibble (I think her top lip was once an elephant trunk :), and I blow a little, and she inhales, unconcerned. She doesn't move away. And she's calm as a cucumber.

Which is one of the amazements to me… that she can want so much, and be so calm and trusting, but that doesn't really translate into crossing thresholds. She has gone to sleep just inches from my chest and it's those moments where I must concentrate on issuing no vibes, no "towards" movements or even thoughts… which has its own issues because when I'm concentrating so hard on not disrupting her trust I know there is anxiety creeping through my every pore :).

The very first day I was in her paddock I lay down on the ground and took a nap. After a bit Benji joined me and dozed off next to me. At some point I heard Noelle's feet drawing close, and I rolled over, chin on my hands. She was about six feet away, head on the ground, wanting to sniff Benji. Intrigued even then.

The fascinating thing to me is still how completely independently wired everything in her brain is working. I can do all of the above… with my left hand when I'm on her right side. But if I so much as lift my right hand to touch her she pulls away. Never mind getting over to her left side. All the trainers and clinicians tell you that whatever you do (training, desensitization, etc) on one side you must also do on the other because horses have monocular vision with each eye when only one eye is on the subject. And they have virtually two separate brains, each getting the feed from each eye. But even so, with horses who have lived their entire lives in domestic care, at least for us, it's never really been like starting from scratch when you move from one side to the other. With Noelle it is. And I've come to believe that the reason is that she has spent six years in the wild having to constantly be on the lookout for predators and she is truly hard-wired to accept no information, on either side, as safe until proven to be so. Consequently, me on one side is totally different than me on the other... until proven to be the same. But that's why we are able to know and love horses today. Because as a prey animal, a flight animal, with no defense against predators except to run, they probably would've never made it to the twenty-first century if they weren't wired the way they are. They would've been extinct eons ago.

Our guys and gals who have spent all of their years in domestic care are genetically the same as those horses in the wild, as Noelle, but they have spent their entire lives, for the most part, learning that me on the right is pretty much the same as me on the left, as long as I don't appear out of nowhere in a flash of light.

I've had many offers of help from folks who have had a lot more experience with Mustangs than I have (none!) and I appreciate them all, but in this adventure I only want one teacher. Miss Noelle. And these daily revelations are why. This should be terrific news to all of you who have dreams of doing something like this but perhaps have felt that you weren't up to the task. You absolutely are. Remember just a bit more than three years ago, Kathleen and I didn't have a horse or a clue. So it can't be rocket science. If I can do it, so can you. You do need a measure of patience. And persistence. You need to commit to doing it on her terms, not yours. But you can do it.

Another reason I want this rank novice, this neophyte, to do this by himself is that I believe in my heart that every horse on the planet wants to be in relationship. With everybody. Remember, as a prey animal the horse's number one concern is safety and security. And both are satisfied when the relationship is good. And if I can reach a good relationship with this Mustang who had never willingly touched or been touched by a human until me, if I can bond with her, and become her leader, then to me that pretty well proves the point. As the New York Times said in an editorial after Barbaro died: *You would have to look a long, long time to find a dishonest or cruel horse. And the odds are that if you did find one, it was made cruel or dishonest by the company it kept with humans. It is no exaggeration to say that nearly every horse – Barbaro included – is pure of heart.*

Did I really believe, in the beginning, that it was going to take this long just to be able to scratch her on the neck... on one side? Probably not. But I did know that I was going to take the time that it takes, and that Noelle would be calling the shots. Not without leadership, where possible and appropriate. But every advance would be her call. That's why I have not put a rope on her, even now when it might be easy to do so. All of our sessions are at liberty.

Would a rope speed up the process? Undoubtedly. Would it harm the relationship in the final analysis? Maybe not. But would she be as willing a partner if I took her choice out of the mix? I doubt it.

In addition to the last three photos, all shot on Day 44, Kathleen shot video on Day 46. Take a look at the difference that just two days can make. She is such an amazing girl and for those of you who have been following our progress you will probably enjoy seeing her thresholds crumbling even as we were taping.

Again, just click on Day 46 in the right hand column on www.thesoulofahorse.com or http://thesoulofahorse.com/blog.

A final note. I'm actually writing this on Day 47, the day after shooting the video, and I started this morning working on her left side with my right hand, completely reversing the setup. It took at least 20 minutes for her to even take a bite of hay and another ten minutes for me to be able to touch her favorite spot, right below her eye. But finally she allowed and I was even able to pick out an eye booger. That's probably all we'll do for a few days because the next four days are supposed to be pouring rain. But I'm very convinced that it will not take as long on the left side as it took on the right. And now I'm wondering, once she accepts my right hand on her left side, will she accept both hands on both sides… or not.

Shhhh, don't tell Kathleen I said that.

It is fascinating.

I think I saw the baby move today.

3

Day 60
OMIGOSH!
SHE'S BAGGING UP!

Dr. Matt was here this morning and dropped a huge bomb. Noelle is bagging up and will probably foal within the next 30 days. I suppose we should've noticed, but this is February 18 and Dr. Matt has been predicting a birth date around June 1.

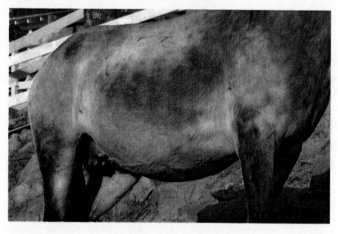

Thirty days from February 18 is *not* June 1.

And she doesn't look *that* pregnant.

At least to these inexperienced eyes.

Holy moly!

The best laid plans and all that. Did I ever tell you that this is our first, as in FIRST, experience with birthing a foal, never mind one from a mustang who has never been touched (willingly) by anyone but me! And just barely at that.

Gleep and gulp!

Even this morning when Dr. Matt got too close Noelle had to pull away from my side.

What if something goes wrong? How will we deal with it?

And my goal from the beginning has been to follow Dr. Robert Miller's Foal Imprinting Program which depends upon my hands being on the foal on its first day of life. I thought I had another three months to get Noelle ready for that. To get our relationship in order. But at this point she doesn't really trust me with herself. Why would she trust me with her baby?

Since the last post I've been able to rub and scratch on both sides as far as her withers, and down each front leg to her knee. This morning on her right side I even reached across her rib cage toward her flank, and she's letting me clean out eye boogers from both eyes.

But all that's at the wrong end if there were to be a problem.

I've begun a bit of halter desensitization, putting just the weight of my hand on the halter loop. But she's nowhere near having a lead rope attached. I've never even been able to touch her without food in my hand. Which I don't think would help much when she's having a baby.

Our shiny new foaling book says we need this long list of stuff, just in case. If we can't get close to her how are we going to use it?

"Take a deep breath, Sweetie. Lower your adrenaline, and pledge to embrace whatever happens calmly and with your brain in gear It'll all be fine."

What would I do without Kathleen?

4

DAY 70
MOLTING NOT FOALING

It's been unseasonably warm the past week and Noelle has been shedding – more like molting – all that long white hair which was helping to keep her warm up in Reno. Underneath a rich golden patina is beginning to emerge.

Today was a good day. Perhaps not the best day Noelle and I have had, but still good. And both of Kathleen's cameras were whirring. Stills and video.

Her left side is still not as comfortable for her as the right, but I think she's doing fantastic.

I've gotten all the way down her front legs to her hoof on both sides, and between her front legs underneath her chest from either side.

Still I can only use my left hand on her right side and my right hand on her left side, which fascinates me. On the right side I've worked my way all the way back to her butt.

Notice the look on her face when I'm back in those "dangerous" zones. Clearly unconcerned. Even less concerned than when I scratch her neck or around her ears. Why? I don't know. But it's interesting. I stay up nights wondering about these things. Also notice that she still looks only barely pregnant, never mind that she's plus or minus twenty days from having a baby.

Even rubbing under her belly brought no reaction. I was trying to feel the baby move but didn't detect a thing. Just a very tight belly. Only after seeing these photos did I realize how calm she was. I, on the other hand, was paying attention to both right-side legs.

I've also been playing with the halter loop, pulling it lightly to the right and to the left. And she is now responding nicely. Not so much to "forward" or "down" but left and right is coming along. See it on the Day 70 video.

Kathleen and I are reading the "foaling book" every night, stacking the information in the book up against what we've seen in the paddock that day. As far as we can tell nothing causes us to believe that Noelle is going to foal anytime soon.

A friend asked us if we had a name for the foal yet. We said we didn't.

He said, "Well, the mom is Noelle. How about Foelle?"

I threatened to publish his email address in the blog.

5

Day 73
It's A Boy!

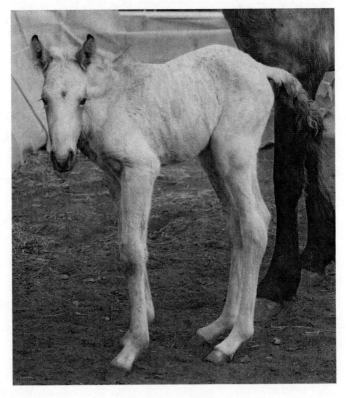

Morning surprise!

For weeks now before assembling the morning feed for the herd on the hill I've been walking down to Noelle's paddock. Just in case. I talk with her for a bit and she usually walks up close to the fence to see if maybe I have any hay in hand.

This morning (I'll never forget the date: March 3rd, 3/3) she was not where she usually hangs out. I walked further down and suddenly my heart caught in my throat. Next to her, flat on the ground lying very still... was a baby. A foal. Joy and fear erupted simultaneously. Why wasn't it moving? I reached for the cell phone, but waited. For the longest time. Quite long enough for me to begin to worry. Finally there was a twitch. A stretch. And this beautiful boy woke up and struggled to his feet.

I called Kathleen.

"We have a baby," I sniveled through building tears.

I heard her screech to the kids, and she hung up.

In seconds they were all at the paddock.

Last night everything was normal. No liquids anywhere. No signs. And this morning there he was. How did she do it without that list of stuff from the foaling book? She didn't even go into the well-padded and protected foaling stall we had built for her. She just did it. Her way. And everything was fine.

God is good.

The next call went to Dr. Matt and he said he'd be right over. The kids were late for school as we all hung out around the paddock for some time. Every camera in the house was clicking or whirring. Watching mommy be very much a mommy. And very protective. Later this morning I went into the paddock and got close enough to take the above photo, but I couldn't touch either one of them, even with a handful of hay. About ten feet was the closest... which was okay because the book says some moms don't accept their babies and it was nice to note such is not the case with Noelle.

It's amazing to see how alert and physically able he is so very early in his life. Dr. Matt estimated that he was born right around 3:00 am, which means these pictures were taken about four hours after his birth. Dr. Matt checked out the birth sack to make sure it

was all there, and then just hung around and watched. And smiled. He sees hundreds of foals a year, but I could tell he likes this boy horse.

I look at the two of them together and am amazed at how he could've fit in there and Noelle look no bigger than she did.

This evening Noelle accepted hay from my hand and I was able to rub her. The foal strolled over to me and I couldn't contain myself. When he was about a foot away – instead of letting him and his curiosity be in control - I reached out to touch and he turned back to mommy. Shame on me. I do know better.

The birth all happened as it does in the wild without human help. And Dr. Matt was very pleased with everything. His confirmation, weight, and temperament (which is very curious).

This baby was conceived in the wild. And yet here he is with us. It's all still mind-boggling. Early in the day he walked over to check out the un-used birthing stall. Noelle grumbled at him to come back but he didn't. He strolled right in. She felt compelled to follow. To protect.

If he's asleep when one of us walks down to the paddock, she paws at him (not so gently) to wake him up. *Get up. We might have to be on the run.* Seems unnecessary to me, but that's her wiring from the wild.

I won't keep you. We're just proud parents wanting to let everyone know. Enjoy the photos from the first day of his life.

(Note: there are several videos from these early days that should be on the website by the time this book is published or very soon thereafter.)

6

MALACHI
THE SOUL OF A HORSE CONTINUES

Malachi's 7th day on the planet.

Malachi is the last book in the Old Testament of the Bible. In Hebrew the word means messenger, and in the Book of Malachi the message is that change is coming.

The prophet Malachi intended to write a book about change. I didn't.

In fact I didn't set out to write a book at all. Kathleen and I were just trying to figure out how to keep and care for a small group of horses that had somehow landed quite unexpectedly in our front yard. We were asking a lot of questions and getting a lot of answers that didn't seem to make any sense. After stumbling through mistake after mistake, amassing an enormous amount of research, and spending a great deal of time with our little herd we discovered that either we were stark raving nuts or there was something very wrong in this world of horses. That's where The Soul of a Horse began.

Thankfully for us it turned out that we weren't nuts. At least not in the clinical sense.

We had little choice but to follow this journey. It was too late to turn back and in truth it held great fascination for me as a storyteller. I've spent most of my life telling stories, usually involving animals, and here we were: two complete neophytes who, a few short months before, didn't have a horse... or a clue. Yet we were leaping face first into uncharted and very controversial waters on a collision course with the ultimate discovery that most "domestic" horses were being kept and cared for in a manner that is diametrically contradictory to their genetic design.

But even at that point, with that knowledge, I was not trying to create a book about change. It was a book about our mistakes, our astonishment at what we were finding, and how somewhere along the journey Kathleen and I both began to realize that what we were learning about relationships, leadership, persistence, and patience didn't apply just to horses.

It seems that part came alive for some. Not a day goes by that we don't hear from readers telling us how the book has changed their lives. People who love horses and people who have never laid hands on a horse. This is all very humbling for us.

The next book (the one you are now reading the Preface for) is the continuation of our journey, the extension of our learning curve, and I suppose, once again, it will be called a book about change. Which is the reason we chose a very special name for our first-ever foal, the offspring of an unhandled pregnant mustang we adopted from the Bureau of Land Management. Considering the death sentence they were both living under – a sentence issued by our federal government – we feel the name is particularly appropriate.

So with all due apologies to my Cash, hero of the *The Soul of a Horse* and author of its Introduction, the next book will belong to a new life on the planet. His name is Malachi... for all the reasons above, and all the reasons to come. – Joe Camp

He's already driving Noelle crazy with his racing and frolicking around the paddock. Wherever he goes, she follows, or tries to. Up and down the hills. Around and around the boulders. Kathleen and I were propped on the fence watching the antics when the above photo was taken.

"Just think of all the foals who don't ever get to do this," she said, "because they're locked up in a stall or some tiny square paddock. It's such a shame."

"Yep," I said. "The foaling book says it'll be okay to let him spend a few hours outside by the end of next week."

"Really?" she laughed, because she knew it was true. "If that's what it says, I think we can make it happen."

Where did we ever get the notion that horses cannot get along without us and our human rules?

I've had a session with Malachi every day since Day 3. Today he's 10 days old (the above photos were taken on Day 7 because Kathleen has been concentrating mostly on video). This is the second day he's worn a halter. He turned tight circles in both directions, backed up a couple of steps, and learned to lead forward in a straight line. Only a few steps at a time, but he was definitely figuring out that a step forward meant release of my light pressure on the halter. I regularly lift and tap all four feet, rub him all over, including his ears, over and around his eyes, and in his nose. I put a finger in his mouth and rub his tongue. And we sit together on a hay bale. He was lying in my lap on his third day of life and already he's almost too big for that (Kathleen promises photos in the next post). He's a rambunctious little bugger and I cannot say that he's in love with his exercises but he's accepting them and trying hard to figure things out. Even while mama hollers next door. I suspect that he'd be doing even better had we been able to isolate him before the third day. It took us that long to figure out how to gain separation. Remember Noelle has never been on a rope and is a very protective mom. We had already built one stall in the paddock where we thought Noelle might want to deliver. She didn't. I spent most of Malachi's second day trying to figure out how to isolate him so I could begin the imprinting process. It was a frustrating mystery until Kathleen said "It's too bad you don't have a remote control for that gate down there."

Bingo.

We had been watching the two of them wander into the "birthing" stall, and eventually Noelle would wander out expecting Malachi to follow. Sometimes he did and sometimes he didn't. If there were a second stall adjacent to the first we could close both horses up in the two stalls, then wait for them to separate and remotely close the gate between them.

"How," Kathleen asked.

"Rig a long line to the gate between the stalls. I can sit in a camping chair up the hill, working on my laptop, waiting for Malachi to wander into the 'play pen' without mama. Then I pull the 'secret' line to shut the gate."

Her look told me it sounded like a Rube Goldberg contraption to her but I believed it would work and time was a-wasting.

Hours later I was propped in my chair just out of camera range up the hill on the left with a neon pink cord looped over my arm... waiting.

And waiting... and waiting.

Meanwhile, Kathleen was having a grand time just watching and shooting video as Malachi romped and played. The magical separation never happened that day, the second day of Malachi's life, and finally I opened the far left gate and let them go wherever they wanted. To encourage more comfort in the stalls I began to place feed in both and soon mama and baby began to wander in and out very casually.

Kathleen had predicted that the foal would be a boy, only because I wanted a girl and had been calling him a her since we first decided to adopt. His boy-ness is probably why I'm approaching all this a bit nervously. I've only been face-to-face with one stallion in my life. And I've never had a hand on a foal prior to Malachi. But I wake up every morning alive and anxious to get back to Mom and babe.

The next morning, Day # 3, it happened. They separated, the gate closed. Noelle bellowed. And my heart felt like it was going to blow right out of my chest. But in a matter of moments my arms were around my new little boy horse. And it was good.

Photos soon.

7

QUALITY TIME

I'm writing this on the 17th day of Malachi's life, but this photo and all the ones below were actually taken on his 13th day. I'm spending so much time with him and Noelle that I'm sorry to say I'm having trouble keeping up with everything else, like photos, newsletters, even email. By the way, all the fantastic photos you'll see in this journal entry were taken by Kathleen. (A big round of applause please :)

The boy is growing so fast we're afraid to blink, afraid we might miss something. Kathleen has shot an enormous amount of video which I haven't been able to edit down and get onto the website yet but hope to do so soon. I think the piece will clearly dramatize how fast he's growing. When he began lying in my lap (on Day 3) we were using two bales of straw but you can see below how On Day 13 he's almost off the far end. Today I had to add a third bale.

The process of lying down begins.

Malachi drifts off into nap-land.

He's such a good boy. Boy for sure, but a good boy. He wore his first halter on Day 9, was leading in circles and taking a few forward steps by the next day, and on Day 11 he was leading every direction on a loose line. Today we had a stroll outside the "playpen" as Kathleen calls it, being careful to never leave mama's sight and she actually handled it well with no snotty remarks :).

Approaching with the lead rope.

No resistance.

Day 13. Leading on loose line.

Kathleen put her foot down and said this boy was not going to wear a pink halter (she ordered blue) so today he finally got to eschew hot pink and take that first walk outside the stall wearing a very handsome marine blue.

Good friend and trick trainer Allen Pogue wouldn't leave us alone until we built a platform. He uses it to give his babies a quiet safe spot to hang out, always near mama, and in very short order his horses will go to any platform or pedestal on a point or cue and stay right there until asked to go somewhere else. So I finally got out the saw and with a little help built Malachi a platform.

He was introduced to it on Day 13, the day these photos were taken. Note Noelle just over my shoulder, taking it all in.

Initially he needed some encouragement, but by the end of the day he was climbing right up on a loose line. He even went up once by himself when my back was turned. I looked back and I swear he was actually beaming with pride. I couldn't keep myself from laughing out loud.

The first several days I spent hours sitting in a camping chair with my laptop waiting for him to go into the playpen, without mama, so I could pull the rope that would close the gate. I've mentioned before that Malachi is so bright I worry about staying ahead of him. Well nothing has changed. Look at the photo below as he takes charge of the "secret" rope that allows me to shut the gate from afar.

As I write this - Day 17 - he already comes to me on his own for a rub and a hug, and if I wrap my arms around him he anticipates lying down in my lap so he relaxes against my body. It's very cool, but if that continues into adulthood it could get a little scary.

He's learning to back up with a shake of the lead rope. Or even a flick of my hands. He worries not a bit when I pick up his feet, or scratch his ears, or put my finger in his mouth. He moves his butt over with the lightest touch and I suspect he'll be doing it with just a point or a look very soon. He's learning at liberty that a light tap on his butt means move forward. On his chest means back up. And he's barely two weeks old.

How does life get better than this? From the day our first three horses came to live with us I've always wondered what it would be like to begin with a horse the day he was born. To never have to wonder about what all might've happened during his first ten years of life. Or why he acts this way or that. To be able to prove my theorem that every horse on the planet would prefer to be in good relationship, even a mustang conceived in the wild. And that a good relationship from day one would breed amazing things. Now if I can just get this strapping young boy to pass the good word on to his mom.

8

TRUST

This photo was taken at 3 weeks old, but our boy horse is almost two months as I write this (see below) and is definitely proving every day that deep down every horse on the planet would prefer to be in relationship than not. Born of two wild unhandled parents he is completely unafraid of people or other horses. Perhaps too much so. I've brought everyone from the herd down at one time or another to see how they respond to Noelle and Malachi. Noelle reads the attitude right away and doesn't approach if she suspects issues – like with Mariah. Mariah is not a snotty horse inside the herd but she wanted absolutely nothing to do with either Noelle or Malachi. Noelle kept her distance but Malachi kept coming, sticking his head through the fence, clicking his mouth "please don't hurt me

I'm just a baby" and each time he did that I had to restrain Mariah with the lead rope to keep her from striking with her mouth. Very unlike her normal behavior. Even Cash was a tad crusty with Malachi although I tend to read it as educational. He had to climb out of his usual easy going demeanor when he was educating Mouse at one year old. That's the only way Mouse would listen, and Cash did a good job. But Malachi is too young for that yet which is probably why mama hasn't started any serious discipline even when he's crawling all over her (see below) or biting her hard on the back of the legs. I, for one, wish she would get on with the discipline thing because it would help me with his desire to bite. I do use discipline, and diversion. Pocket and Mouse were both very sweet with Noelle and Malachi (see below). They all did lots of nose sniffing and blowing, and both Pocket and Mouse were very gentle with Mal. BTW, the rail fence you can see at the very top right corner of the above photo is the gate into the hillside pasture where the herd lives, which is why this is Noelle's favorite place to hang out because she can exchange looks and greetings with the other horses whenever one approaches the gate.

3 Weeks
Feels So Good!

3 Weeks – Pestering Mama

25 Days

Note the loose lead line. This is the first time Malachi was lead out of the "playpen" (Kathleen's name for the stall where the early training and imprinting was done). Here we're over by the paddock fence, maybe 30 or 40 feet away from the playpen… and maybe 50 feet away from mama. Scary new territory, and probably the farthest he has ever been away from his mom. But he was more curious than worried. And trusting completely, leading wherever we went on a loose line.

Both of these photos were also taken on his 25th day. He loves to play and frolic but note that I've taken a step away, not fully trusting his control of those flying feet.

I love this shot – also from Day 25 - because most of my work with him is like this, at liberty. No line. Sometimes he steps up onto the pedestal all by himself to peer over the corral rail at Noelle, even when he's free to use the gate to get to her. I can almost hear him saying *Look at me mommy. Look how tall I am!* Stepping onto pedestals (or into trailers) is something he'll never be worried about as an adult. Many thanks to Allen Pogue for pressing this point with me.

Four and a half weeks old

What a pretty boy!

Out in the free world

7 weeks old

Our canine superstar Benji, Oprah's favorite onscreen animal, has never had anything to do with any of our horses. Not even sweet Cash. Until Malachi was born. From the very first day Benji was intrigued. Perhaps because she was rescued from a shelter and, in a way, so was Malachi. Benji promotes adoption and so will Malachi. They must realize they're kindred spirits. Their antics getting to know each other were captured in an online video. Just Google: *Benji Gets a New Baby...Horse.*

Malachi's seven-week-old birthday present was to get outside
in the free world at liberty. No halter or lead rope. Twice a day. I
load the Gator every morning and evening to feed the herd on the
other side of the hill and the feed-prep shed is right by Malachi's
playpen. So now he gets to come out and play while I'm prepping
the feed and loading the Gator. He never goes far and usually is
stealing hay from the Gator. I rub him and play with his feet and
teach him little things. When it's time to go back in a few nudges
and finger points will normally do it. Sometimes Noelle calls him
back. If he ignores her she'll leave without him and that always
does the trick.

First time out at liberty – seven weeks old

Once again, many thanks to Kathleen for the gorgeous photography. I think she's found a new career. Who'd of thought a lawyer
would have such a nice eye :)

9

MORNING ADVENTURE

What a spectacular morning! Malachi really stretched his boundaries on his at-liberty walkabout. Although today it was more of a race-about.

When he first came out for his liberty time I introduced him to a small red ball that was designed to enable a horse to pick it up. Never thinking that he would figure it out the first time, I called him over and gave him a taste.

He nibbled on it for a few moments. The ball is very cleverly designed. Allen Pogue, the trick trainer who was the focus of Chapter 24 in *The Soul of a Horse* had sent it to me for Malachi. It's a perfect sphere that will roll like any other ball but the circumference of the sphere is molded with the legs of an octagon, each leg being a soft rubber handle which the horse can actually grasp with his teeth and hold on.

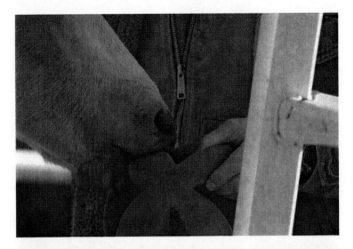

He was so proud of himself when he actually did pick it up and hold it all by himself that leaped straight up like a jack-in-the-box and kicked at the air.

He had never ventured farther than the far end of our tack room (which is right next to the hay shed where I load the Gator for the hillside herd feeding) but his adrenaline was up now and without a blink he loped right past the tack room, 50 yards down a steep path, around a sharp turn, and into our arena.

This was his first trip ever into the arena. He raced from one end to the other a couple of times, then raced back up to the tack room. I stepped toward him and he wheeled and raced (I mean RACED) down the little road back into the arena, then back out and up. Very proud of himself. I decided not to give him the opportunity to learn that he could run away from me so I just ignored him when he was close by... and watched with a big smile when he was down in the arena. He wasn't on guard or worried at all. Just curious. This was his time, and I relaxed and enjoyed watching his little brain at work figuring things out. He must've run the full circuit from tack room down the road to the far end of the arena 8-10 times. One trip he missed the gate into the arena and did a perfect slide stop at the fence. Then stepped around the gate and took off again to the far end. Mama was pretty much beside herself at first and I loved it that I was up near her and she could see that I had nothing to do with all this. She would go down into the lower stall (which overlooks the arena) and watch Malachi racing around, often squealing at him, then she would trot back up and look at me as if to say: Aren't you going to do something?? *It's your baby,* says I.

Finally Malachi nosed around the outside of the arena and discovered the shortcut path up to the lower stall where Noelle was monitoring it all. He trotted right up the path (the cell phone photo above - the edge of the arena can be seen down the hill) and hung out with mom across the stall fence for a bit. I was just before going over to urge him back toward home when he started climbing up the *wrong* way. I held my breath as he wriggled through a very narrow space between the tall rocky hill and the lower stall then climbed straight up the rocks back to the far side of his playpen. With a single point from me he trotted right into the playpen, into mom's stall, and started nursing, quite the proud little boy. Well, not so little. A few minutes later he was back at the closed gate asking me if he could come out again. Maybe later, I said, and gave him a couple of rubs and a treat, then headed out to feed the herd on the other hillside.

While watching him race back and forth I kept thinking about the statement Kathleen had made when Malachi was galloping circles around the paddock. "Just think of all the foals locked up in stalls who never get to do this."

His feet, by the way, look sensational. No need for any trimming yet.

Today Malachi is two months and two days old… And BIG! This photo was taken two days ago.

10

WHY MUSTANGS?

Below is a portion of a chapter from the next book, which might give you a hint as to why we adopted Noelle, who was pregnant with Malachi when we brought her home. And why the next book is becoming a passionate exploration into the soul of a mustang. Those in our care, and those in the wild.

So there I was, face to face with the facts: genetically speaking there was really no difference between a horse living in the wild and a so-called domesticated horse. What each horse has learned from his or her environment is obviously different, as I would soon come to understand. But their genetic ability to live successfully in the wild is the same.

Which is how Kathleen and I found ourselves on that collision course with the ultimate discovery that our horses - *most* "domestic" horses - were being kept and cared for in a manner that is contra-dictory to their genetic design.

But there was good news in the realization.

We had in our care perhaps the only species on the planet that lives with humans but could boast its own living laboratory in the wild. No more need for guess work. These wild horses could reveal the truth, be a road map to the way horses were designed to live. A way that works because they have survived for millions and millions of years.

If it hadn't worked so well we would've never heard of the horse.

God and Mother Nature knew what they were doing. Horses were designed over time through trial and error to live and eat and move in certain ways; and the study of all of this could provide more incredibly valuable information about how we should be feeding, keeping, and caring for the horses we choose to associate with than has ever been understood before.

So I was astonished when I learned that we were at risk of losing America's wild horses. How could that be? These horses are not only a living laboratory, as a group they are a legendary icon of the American west; sentient beings that are part of our national soul.

But the wild horse is also at the very heart of a range war with his demise as the ultimate goal. It all has to do with control of public lands across the western states. The BLM and the National Forest Service administer the 55 million acres that have been designated by law to be devoted principally to the welfare of wild horses and burros. According to Craig Downer, Ph.D. in Wildlife Ecology, these two government agencies disregarded the law and reduced that 55 million acres by approximately 36% and then leased more than 95% of the remaining to cattle and sheep ranchers.

Making matters worse, these ranchers convinced the government to allow them to hunt and eliminate the cougar and the wolf because these two predators were killing and eating their cattle and sheep. The cougar and the wolf, like the wild horse, are historically indigenous species that are supposed to be living under the protection of the government on federal lands. The cougar and the wolf are also the natural predators of the wild horse, so without these predators in place, the herds multiply much faster than they would otherwise. Multiply much faster into a world where their forage and water is being consumed by cattle and sheep that effectively outnumber them by more than 150 to one. On land that by law is to be *devoted principally* to the welfare of wild horses and burros.

So rather than removing the cattle and sheep which would allow the horse to once again be the principle presence on the land and allow the cougar and wolf to flourish and allow natural balance to return, the BLM has stated to the media that the land will not support the number of wild horses and burros living on it so their numbers must be reduced. At this writing more than 33,000 mustangs have been captured and put in holding pens around the country. Not because the land will not support 60,000 horses but because it will not support that many horses plus at least a million for-profit cattle and sheep.

Kathleen and I were in a fog of déjà vu. Like when we discovered how the horse was really supposed to live, and how damaging life in a stall wearing metal shoes and eating sugar coated meals can be to the physical and emotional health of the horse. Once again we were feeling that we had to be nuts. If all this were true wouldn't people know about it? Wouldn't they act on the knowledge? Surely we were missing something.

There's more.

The ranchers were not satisfied with being able to lease the land for well under the market value of comparable privately held land. Nor were they satisfied with being able to hunt the natural predators of the horse. They wanted the wild horses off the land entirely. Many of these ranchers were actively attempting to get the 1971 law repealed by trying to convince the government, the media, and the lay public that the horses don't belong on these lands because they are not native. Not indigenous. The federal government is only obligated to protect native wildlife. Their claim was that the mustang is merely feral. Domesticated horses that had escaped from the Spanish, the Indians, and the cavalry. Feral like the cats who leave home to live in the back alleys of New York.

Their claim simply ignores the historic and scientific truth in pursuit of financial gain.

The wild horse is as native and indigenous to North America as the Bengal tiger is to India or the lion is to Africa. The wild horse was born here in the region that was to become Idaho, Utah and Wyoming and fully evolved over a period of 52 million years. Approximately 10,000 years ago an unknown cataclysm wiped out the horse in North America along with numerous other species apparently including the saber-toothed tiger. But not before the horse had migrated across the Bering Strait Land Bridge and spread to the rest of the world. Then in the early sixteenth century the horse was re-introduced to his homeland by the Spanish Conquistadores.

He became what is termed *reintroduced native wildlife.*

If for some reason a plague wiped out the tiger in India and the species was re-introduced from, say, wild animal park inventory that had originally come from India would those tigers be considered native, indigenous?

Or feral?

Absolutely the former.

Remains of the earliest animal anywhere in the world to bear recognizably horse-like anatomy were found in the Idaho-Utah-Wyoming area dating 52 million years ago.

Dating three-and-a-half million years ago the now famous fossils found near Hageman, Idaho represent the oldest remains of the fully evolved genus Equus, roughly the size and weight of today's Arabian horse. At this time the horse had not yet migrated across the Bering Strait Bridge.

Bones found recently in North America from horses that are dated one million years ago appear indistinguishable from Equus Caballus (the modern day domestic horse).

And studies of DNA sequences taken from long bone remains of horses found preserved in the Alaskan permafrost deposits dated 12,000 to 28,000 years ago differ by as little as 1.2% from modern counterparts.

When the Spanish brought the horse to America they were bringing him home. Back to his native land. Wearing the same genetics, the same DNA sequencing he was wearing when he left and when those left behind were wiped out.

Some wildlife groups consider the bighorn sheep and the American bison "native" to North America. However, both species actually evolved in Asia and came into North America via the Bering Strait Land Bridge. The horse, Equus caballus, conversely, evolved exclusively in North America and crossed the Bering Strait bridge into Siberia, traveling in the other direction. Equus caballus was fully evolved on the North American continent and was migrating west well before the cataclysm of 10,000 years ago.

So conversation that leads anyone to believe that the wild horse is anything other than "reintroduced native wildlife" is folly. Or worse yet malevolent.

As I write this the 33,000 wild mustangs residing in government holding pens and facilities around the country amount to more than half of all the remaining wild mustangs in existence.

And those remaining in the wild are living below viable levels. Which simply put means below the number that must be available for breeding to keep the horse from not being forced into incest for the species to attempt to survive.

All because of those cattle and sheep. Illegal cattle and sheep. To allow all this to happen someone had to knowingly break the 1971 law.

I was astounded. And embarrassed that I didn't know any of this before.

And sad.

Made sadder when I learned that the Government Accountability Office was recommending death for the 33,000 wild mustangs in government custody because it was costing too much to feed and care for them.

The OED definition of *domestication* scratched and clawed its way back into my consciousness.

To civilize.

OED's assumption of course was that humans would be doing the civilizing.

Maybe humans are the ones needing it.

11

THE BUCKSKIN EMERGES

Not only does Malachi continue to grow (I had to raise the plank that keeps Noelle out of his playpen this week) his whiteness is now giving way to the buckskin underneath. Especially on his *neck (See the darkening areas on his neck and rump)*. Kathleen doesn't usually get to show up in these posts because she's always behind the camera... but she figured that out in the shot above :)

These were taken yesterday afternoon just outside his playpen while we were mixing and loading the gator to feed the pasture five. Every morning and evening while we're loading up, Malachi gets to wander out in the free world wherever he wants, which is usually not far. He hasn't yet made a second trip down to the arena like the one described in the last newsletter. Dr. Matt is just amazed at how big and strong he's getting and how good he looks... and how many stallion tendencies he's already showing (he'll be 3 months old on June 3rd – my how time flies). So we're sorry to say that on Thursday he will lose his manhood. It had to happen sometime as we have no intention of breeding and want him to be able to live a good life with the herd. Still, he's going to be such a big good looking boy that it makes me sad to do it.

I have to be a bit more careful when working with him these days because now when I get a foot under his hoof it hurts!

Noelle and I have pretty much been treading water since Malachi's birth. I've just been trying to maintain, and not let her slide backwards. Serious work needs full attention and with Malachi around she's either very annoyed with his pestering, or worried about him if he gets too far away or is locked out. As you might remember, we left her with me rubbing her pretty much all over with one hand while she ate hay from my other hand. Recently I decided to trade places and let her do the touching. I stand right by her tub of chopped salad (Safe Starch forage) and hold out my hand for her to touch and sniff. The idea was that as soon as she did, I'd walk away so she could eat. The first time she didn't like it at all. To eat, she'd have to get closer to me than she ever had without food in my hand. The first time, she took a step back, blinked a couple of times, then stepped right up and sniffed my hand. I told her how good she was and left her to eat. Now it's a ritual. She knows how to get rid of me :) But because she's making the choice to do it and "stretching her envelope," I can now walk right past her tub and she just swings her head away to let me pass, instead of jumping back several steps like she used to do. Not a big advance, but an advance. And it's fun to watch her brain whirling and spinning.

The last photo ever taken with Malachi and his Mom.

12

A Brilliant Star
Extinguished

Our Hearts are Breaking

On the evening of June 3rd, exactly three months from the day of his birth, we lost Malachi in the aftermath of a violent thunder and lightning storm that knocked out a power pole on our property. As we piece together what happened, a fleet of huge power company trucks climbed our driveway that night which passes right by Noelle and Malachi's paddocks and stalls. These gigantic loud monsters apparently freaked Malachi into a frenzy and he cracked his head on a post or stall rail. According to Dr. Matt he dropped immediately and died on the spot. We are devastated. Just devastated. He was our first and only baby. We only wanted one. And so much of the rest of my life was wrapped up in him. I so looked forward to going down at feeding times because Malachi got to come outside and play while I loaded the gator for the pasture feed. He was such a good boy. And so big, and strong, and healthy. And smart, and willing. Everything you could ask for in a messenger for the mustangs; and he represented everything we had learned in The Soul of a Horse, our entire journey. His birth was to be the fore-word of the next book. I loved him so, and so looked forward to the rest of my life with my boy horse. It was all so random. So wrong. I can't stop crying. I am lost.

The photo above was taken on May 24th. The first four below on May 25th and are the last ones taken with me when he was fully awake. The next two were the very last ones taken, on May 28th, the day of his gelding.

I will be offline and journal entries and posts will be on hold for a while.

Joe

Goodbye Malachi, my boy horse. I don't know
what I will do without you.

13

LOVED

Twenty-four days after Malachi's death I finally went back to the keyboard.

Kathleen and I want to thank all of you who posted comments, sent emails and cards of condolence, prayers, and warm thoughts after the tragic death of our beloved Malachi. I must admit to you that I have so far only read the barest few of the hundreds that came in. But we intend to read every one at some point – when we're a bit less fragile – and we'll attempt to answer every one personally.

We're beginning the long climb out of the hole, assisted in no small way by having to focus on Noelle's loss as well as our own, and her new-found need for companionship. I have no idea what I'll be blogging about as our journey continues but hopefully it will be of benefit to everyone as we all try to make our way through the classroom of real life. Once again, I can't tell you how special and loved you have made us feel as we have struggled through this awful time in our lives. Thank each of you very, very much.

Joe & Kathleen

14

RISING FROM THE ASHES

For those who wonder whether horses grieve let me assure you that
they do. Noelle's demeanor has changed completely since the loss
of Malachi. She wanted – needed – companionship and I was the
only one around. We helped each other. Consoled each other. Re-
assured each other. And the net result for both of us has been to
watch thresholds fall away at an ever increasing pace.

After June 3rd, she was so out of character, moving from one
place to another, spending enormous amounts of time standing
over the spot where Malachi was born. It just broke my heart.

I had never been able to approach and touch her without feed
in my hand, but one day, with tears in my eyes from watching her
move from one uncomfortable spot to another, I went into the
paddock empty handed and walked up to her. At the very last minute she backed away, just a couple of steps. I wanted so to wrap my
arms around her and bury my tears in her neck. To explain that I
knew how she felt and how very, very sorry I was. But of course, I
did none of that. I just turned around, my back to her, and stood
quietly. It was only a few seconds before she was standing quietly
right beside me. Then her forehead touched my arm, pressed
against it, and she remained there for a very long time. This was
where she wanted to be. She wanted, needed, the companionship.
And Kathleen just happened to be there with her camera. I return
to this picture often because it was a very special moment. Horses
rarely *need* humans, which is why relationship created out of choice
is so important.

Since that moment I have been able to approach her virtually anywhere at any time. Without food. And make contact.

A couple of mornings later while I was mucking her paddock, she offered up a perfect "join up"… she walked right up behind me and nosed my shoulder. I turned and rubbed her forehead, took a couple of steps and she followed, licking and chewing. This is the first time ever that she had done the approaching.

Now, when she's munching Safe Starch in her open stall, I'll stand for 10-15 minutes at a time pulling tangles out of her mane while she munches. Using both hands… on her left side (you might remember that this was her "scariest" side).

The first time I took a grooming brush into the stall she freaked out. Wouldn't get close to it. So I left it on a straw bale in Malachi's play pen and surrounded it with alfalfa :)

Two mornings later the brush was on the ground, as was Malachi's red ball and the stick he used to teethe on. That morning I took the brush in while Noelle was eating and she got her first ever brushstrokes on her neck. I can now brush all the way back to her butt on both sides.

My hand is welcome down to her front left knee before she gets nervous.

When she does freak at something, it's now shorter-lived. She comes back quicker, might only be a step or two instead of halfway to Alaska.

About a week ago Kathleen and I put two folding chairs in the play pen (12×20) where she is now getting most of her small condiment of alfalfa… and every evening after loading the Gator for the hillside herd feed, we settle into the chairs with a small jelly glass of wine and chat about the day (no agenda whatsoever)… as Noelle nibbles alfalfa at our feet, pokes her nose into our faces for a whiff, checks out the dirty jeans, and tries to buddy up with Benji. After the feed is gone, she'll usually just hang out with us, foot cocked, watching the birds bombard the apricot tree.

Last night she was sniffing and blowing in my nose so closely that her muzzle hairs were tickling the inside of my nose. It was so cool.

After a bit she wandered over to Malachi's platform and sniffed around the top where Malachi would stand and look over the stall rail at her. We couldn't hold back the tears.

She has a way to go, especially in the area of pressure on the halter, but she's made more progress in the past few weeks than in all the months preceding. It's still not easy to sit in the play pen without thinking about Malachi, and Kathleen and I both sort of lost it last night for a time. But these gains with Noelle are wonderful and the night ended with Kathleen receiving her very first touch from Noelle and her very first permission to rub. We're both trying to stay focused on these positives, once again learning – at the graduate school level – the amazing rewards that patience will reap. And learning again to trust in ourselves.

15

LIKE SON, LIKE MAMA

Patience has never been my long suit. And the ability to panic at the least little thing seems to be embedded in my genetics. So maybe you can imagine what was going on in my tummy the morning that Noelle, our unhandled wild mustang, decided she would take a walkabout out in the free world.

Like son like mama. Malachi, her baby, often had liberty time outside his playpen when we were loading the Gator to feed the herd on the hillside. He just wandered around freely, stealing hay from the Gator, getting a rub or a scratch, pretty much whatever he wanted to do. Until one day he decided to go exploring (see Chapter 9 – Morning Adventure). After a freak storm-related accident killed him I would often leave the gate to his playpen open, just for emotional reasons. For me. Wishing he would walk through just once more... and certain that as nervous and freaky about new things as Noelle was she would never venture out through the gate.

I couldn't have been more wrong.

I was piling hay in the Gator a few mornings ago when a strange sound turned me around and there she was... standing on the driveway. Keep in mind that even though she is finally allowing a bit of grooming, even combing of her mane, she has never worn a lead rope, nor has she been led in any fashion. I gulped – a big one – squished my adrenaline down as far as it would squish and said to myself *Okay, what now?*

At the moment she had the upper hand. There was no angle I could achieve that would direct her back into the playpen, so clearly this was going to be an adventure. I found it fascinating that she was so calm. Usually the slightest change would bring on a wide-eyed spell of huffing and puffing. Move one feed tub to the other side of the stall and you'd think a cougar had just walked in. But here she was, out where she had never been before, and she was as calm as a cucumber. And very curious. She looked up at the house, high on the hill above her.

Oh no, I thought.

There's a very steep hill of boulders behind the house. If she got off down that hill she would not be safe and there would be very little I could do to direct her back up.

**When this photo was taken I had no idea
that she was planning a walkabout.**

I attempted to calmly slide around behind her and get a better angle… just as she decided to have a look-see at that structure up on the hill from which we were always coming and going. At one time or another all of our horses have been loose within the perimeter fence, but only one of them, my Cash, has ever been brave enough to venture up the narrow drive behind the garage.

Now there were two. Cash and this wild mustang.

I sprinted up the steps to the front door, a wad of alfalfa in one hand, slipped through the house to the back door, and eased out onto the driveway just moments before she reached the edge of the hill. Paying careful attention to body language, hers and mine, and talking softly, I walked up slowly and offered her a bite of alfalfa while cutting off her access to the hill. She sniffed it but didn't eat. Then she turned and quite calmly ambled off back down the driveway. This walkabout was becoming a terrific learning experience, hopefully for both of us. I followed her down without agenda other than attempting to subtly control her direction by turning and twisting my body. I've forgotten which clinician painted this picture but it works: pretend that a long pole is extended from your belly button. Wherever you put the end of that pole will affect the direction your horse moves. Noelle wanted to climb onto the lawn in front of the house but a twist of my torso past her drive line put the end of the imaginary pole right by her left eye and she calmly turned back onto the driveway. She stopped. I stopped. After a bit of sniffing, I clucked, and took a step forward. She walked on. This was becoming fun.

Kathleen had seen Noelle leaving the playpen from the kitchen window and was already out with the video camera. Here I am with a loose mustang and she's not thinking how to help, but which camera to grab. I asked her to block the pathway to the hillside pasture where the rest of our herd resides. The concern was that if Noelle managed to get over to that pasture to socialize with the other horses there would be no way to get her back without a lot of raised adrenaline levels. So far this had been an interesting and good experience for all concerned. I hoped we could keep it that way.

Sure enough as Noelle rounded the garage and spotted the pathway to the hillside pasture she began to trot straight for it. Kathleen did her "calm cougar" imitation and Noelle turned at the last minute and started up the front steps to the house. To my knowledge she had never been on a step before. The steps fork and I had no choice but to hurry to block her option to the right, which would lead to the steep hill behind the house. She weighed her remaining options. Either leap over the stone wall to get around me, or go on up several more flights of steps. I offered her my standard greeting, a bite of alfalfa. She contemplated, thus relaxed a bit, then turned fully around and moved off down the steps. This was her freakiest moment as she sorted out navigating down the eight steps. Kathleen was still blocking the path to the pasture so she wandered off down the driveway, unfortunately past the entrance to the playpen. I chose not to follow because to push her into a dead-end at our property gate would be to likely cause her to make a bad decision. I waited.

Eventually she wandered back up and I calmly pointed to the right while blocking her other options. She took the point but ignored the playpen gate, instead wandering off through our "covered bridge" to the tack room then down a very steep hill to our small arena.

Kathleen shot video and I just watched for a while as she wandered around the arena sniffing here and there. She had watched Malachi's every move from her stall – with frustration – the day he made the same trip.

She didn't appear to have any immediate plans to come back up so I ambled down, went in, and offered her a bite of alfalfa. This time she took a bite, then I slid off behind her and urged her to move back up the hill. When she reached the steepest point she broke into a lope and tossed a playful kick off to one side. That brought a smile. She was having fun.

At the top of the hill she dropped right back into a curious walk sniffing her way through the covered bridge whereupon she met Kathleen with her arms spread wide, a handy stick in each hand, projecting at least a twelve foot wide profile. No waving. No noise. Just body direction. When I rounded the corner huffing and puffing from the climb Noelle was walking calmly back into the playpen. I followed her in, closing – and <u>locking</u> – the gate. She nibbled a bite of alfalfa from my hand and got a few kind words, and the event was over. Without incident. And with very little to-do or raised adrenaline levels.

I was very proud of Kathleen. At that moment in time she had barely touched Noelle. And was very aware of how extremely freaky she could be on occasion. To keep her head, to stay calm and focused and just go with the flow was difficult enough for me, but a monumental challenge for Kathleen who has a "flight instinct" that, at times, could match Noelle's. But in the end, Kathleen is the one who quietly directed Noelle back home. And I didn't even get to see exactly how she did it. What moves she made. And, beautifully, she doesn't remember. Which means her experience is turning into instinct. Yippee!

It was a terrific lesson for all of us. Noelle learned that we could cause her to move wherever we wanted her to move. And she allowed us to do so, which is the very essence of herd leadership. Who moves who.

Kathleen and I learned with clarity that keeping your head works. That being calm and thinking a problem through works. That patience works. As Pat Parelli says *taking the time that it takes* works. In spades. Whether you're out on a walkabout with a wild mustang or solving a problem in your everyday life.

Good girl Noelle. Thank you.

16

LICKED BY A HORSE

I have never been licked by a horse before. Lots of sniffing, nudging, lip nibbling, and just hanging out close by. But never a full-blown, full-tongue lick on the arm. Especially by a mustang who's never even had a lead rope on. Yesterday I was licked. Kathleen and I (and ALL of the dogs) were sitting in the play pen having our evening no-agenda talk time while Noelle munched hay all around us. Benji was at my feet and Noelle was making her daily attempt to strike up a relationship but Benji hasn't warmed up to her like she did with Malachi.

Maybe Noelle's size plays into it. But when Noelle tried to get a nose sniff, Benji leaped up into my lap. She obviously felt safer there because she allowed Noelle to get closer. But it was a surprise when Noelle reached out and licked Benji's ear, spitting out the hairs almost one at a time.

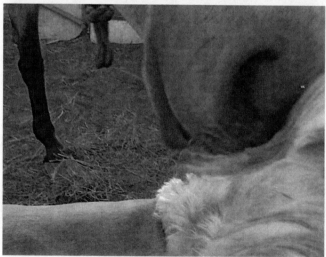

I was watching closely to make sure teeth weren't emerging, and they weren't, so I turned to make sure Kathleen was taking this in, and felt this warm wet thing on my wrist. Lick... lick... lick. Followed by the click... click... click of Kathleen's cell phone camera.

Unfortunately Kathleen was locked in her chair, trying not to scare Noelle, so she had very little maneuverability. And she was using a cell phone so these are not her best photos but perhaps you can get a sense of what was going on. Just amazing stuff.

It was weird, and I wondered aloud if it might be a salt issue. It had been very hot that day and I'm sure I tasted salty. Noelle gets a granular salt/mineral supplement with her other goodies in the morning but for some reason I had never put out a free-choice tub where she could take what she wanted whenever she wanted it. I amended that immediately and now Malachi's little baby-food tub is a fixture in the play pen. But this got me thinking about the salt/mineral blocks we used to use back in the beginning (almost four whole years ago now). And a poll I recently read on The-Horse.com asking how many folks still use blocks. I was astounded at the number.

One of the many things I asked about when our first three horses landed in our yard was, "Aren't we supposed to have a salt block?" "Of course," was the unanimous answer. Can't hurt." The reason it's in a block, we were told, is so the horse can't get too much. *You know how bad salt can be for high blood pressure and other things.* We bought it because that's all the information we had. That was before we learned that horses are quite good at monitoring what they need and ingesting enough to cover their needs if given the option to do so. And it was before we learned how much horses need their salt, especially under certain pasture conditions. And before we discovered that the problem with salt and mineral blocks is that there is no way most horses can "lick" enough of what they need from a block because the horse, unlike the cow, does not have a sandpaper tongue to scrape away the goodies locked in the block. These blocks were originally designed for cattle and they more or less migrated into the horse world. A horse simply cannot do enough licking to serve the needs of his body. Now I've discovered that even the cow can't get enough out of a block during times of acute need. Dr W. W. Swerczek, DVM, PhD says: *"Most cattlemen assume they have adequate sodium if cattle are exposed to salt blocks. Cattle and other herbivores cannot obtain enough salt or sodium from hard salt blocks during periods of acute needs. The most dominant animals in a herd will horde a salt block and the remainder will leave without any salt. Even the animals that horde the block cannot consume enough salt to neutralize the acute excessive dietary nitrate during periods of acute stress to forages, like frosts and freezes to high nitrogenous forages."*

Dr. Matt, our vet, says that he's seen many a small block chewed to pieces because that's the only way the horse can attempt to get enough of what he needs from the block. Also he sees a lot of folks depending upon the ingredients in sacked feeds to supply what their horses need. The problem with that is: a standard portion of any sack feed doesn't take into consideration the differences in the metabolism of each animal, the differences in the way they are living, their stress levels, or the differences in times of the calendar year.

Study after study says it's best to leave it up to the horses. They will know when they need it and how much they need. So I would definitely recommend that yours have access to a free-choice-all-the-time granular salt and trace mineral mix. We have two buckets hanging from the pasture fence. Our pasture-five have access to them 24/7. And now Noelle has her little tub. We use Dr. Dan Moore's formulation called Red Cal because we like what we read about the product, and what we read about him... *and* because the mix will last through several rains and still be viable. Just let it settle a bit after a rain and pour off the liquid. What's left in the bucket is still good to go. But there are also many different formulations out there easily found via a Google search and all are better than forcing your horse to attempt to supply his needs by licking on a block. Or your wrist :)

17

NEVER PRAY FOR PATIENCE
GOD WILL GIVE YOU A HORSE

I know I keep saying that patience is not a concept I've had much contact with. But like so many homo sapiens, I want everything to happen right now. I think it's genetic. The shortest distance has always been a straight line. We humans tend to be that way. Especially in this millennium of instant gratification. But since my introduction to horses, I've come to learn that the good stuff just doesn't happen that way. Whether it's your horse, your dog, your business, or your life it doesn't spin on a dime. You cannot snap your fingers and have your way. The right stuff takes time.

At this point Kathleen is laughing hysterically because she knows my history with the "p" word. She probably suspects that I can't even spell it. Or couldn't until I met up with horses. They're still teaching me with every encounter. Especially that mustang, Miss Noelle.

I thought I had, at last, become a student of *patience* through our early work with the "Hillside Herd". Then Noelle arrived and informed me that I hadn't even scratched the surface. Thankfully the lessons she teaches also apply to every other horse on the planet, and to everything else I'm doing in life. As virtually every clinician I've ever encountered says: *Take the time that it takes and it'll take less time.* The way my parents used to say it is*: Why is there always enough time to do it again after you've done it wrong, but there's never enough time to do it right in the first place?*

All of this bubbled up yesterday when I stumbled onto the video of Day #18 with Noelle (Chapter 2). Her 18th day with us back in early January of this year. I had not yet touched her and she had not yet eaten from my hands. Thankfully Kathleen had her point-and-shoot camera down in the paddock and had shifted it into the video mode. I remembered grumbling to myself that day: *Why is she still shooting? It's a waste of time! Nothing – I mean NOTHING – is going on!*

But watching the video I realized how wrong I was. To view this video in its entirety is to never forget one terrific lesson in patience… and persistence. To watch this wild mustang, who had never touched or willingly been touched by any human, who had spent all but a few months of her six years of life in the wild with her family herd, to study her eyes and body language is to see a horse who wanted so badly to come to me, to be in relationship, to have a bite of what I was offering, but quite simply could only go so far. Could only progress an inch at a time. This was not free-choice decision making. It was hard-wired fear from a lady who had been taught from the moment she was born to suspect everything. Flee first and ask questions later. To understand this, to understand what she was saying, was to understand from whence she came. And that understanding filled me with what I needed to hang in there. To stick with it. To not get antsy and blow it. To leave the decision entirely up to her. To prove to her that I could be trusted when she – not I – worked it out.

To be patient.

As mentioned before, if you can last through this video, it will be something you won't soon forget. *Holy moly. This is excruciating!* But that means the message will be something you won't soon forget either. I urge you to give it a watch. You might never have a mustang… but the concept applies to every horse, every dog, every encounter, and all of your life. Just look for Day 18 with Noelle in the right-hand column of the website or blog.

Noelle eats from my hand for the first time.

18

Onward into the Future

The preceding chapter was written almost two months after that fateful June 3rd that ripped our lives apart. We were working our way into the future, step by step, trying to stay focused on the continuing journey, trying to regain meaning and relevance in our lives and our communication with you. I still had not read most of emails and posts and none of the cards and letters sent to us throughout this time. Neither had Kathleen.

As I write this now, attempting to wrap up the first of three sections in this book, it's almost a year and a quarter later and I'm amazed what a short period of time these pages covered chronologically. It doesn't feel that way at all. The memories stretch on and on and seemingly could fill a hundred volumes, not merely a hundred pages. And to be sure there is so much missing. But the tears streaming down my face confirm that it'll all have to wait. Maybe that's why *Who Needs Hollywood* and this blog book slipped in between *The Soul of a Horse* and its follow-up. Maybe God knew I needed the time.

My mind is flooded with the wealth of Kathleen's photographs, all spinning and turning and pushing through my head like they were controlled by some elaborate computer program. But there's one that keeps coming back to the forefront, and it's not of Malachi, but of Noelle. I'm so happy that Kathleen caught this moment because I so thoroughly identify with it. I do the same thing. All the time. Even now.

I close my eyes and see him on that platform. I open them and he's not there. And I don't understand. Any more than Noelle did when this photograph was taken.

The platform was already well-worn, and weighed a ton, and could've been rebuilt much less expensively than it cost to move it across the country.

But it came with us to Tennessee.

PART TWO

DIFFERENT WORLDS

19

ESCAPING TAXAFORNIA

This was no easy decision. It was overflowing with complexities and angst. Kathleen had lived her entire life in southern California. All of her immediate family is here. And half of mine, the other half in Montana. So the notion of moving to middle Tennessee left a few chords unstruck. I'm not assuming that any of you really care where we hang our hats, but looking back on the process I believe we learned a few extremely valuable lessons. No one is more surprised than we are that we actually did it, that we actually evaluated the situation, made a plan, executed it, and here we are, at least six months later at the other end, a bit stunned that we really got this far. That we actually took charge of our lives before things began to crumble around us. And we are more convinced than ever that our move is the correct thing to do.

We had talked for years about escaping the high costs of California once the twins were out of high school, which is now a little less than two years away. But the last set of tax and utility hikes caused me to begin doodling with some financial projections. Then the bottom dropped out of the stock market and took our retirement fund with it. Suddenly we were facing the fact that we might not make it to the twins' graduation unless we got busy and found financing for another movie. Gleep! Never been faced with such before. And at that moment, with the economy in the tank, financing another movie was probably not even possible. Never mind that I really wasn't ready to do another movie yet. A production takes the better part of two years out of your life, most of it 24/7, literally working around the clock. And I mean work. No matter what you've heard, most of the movie-making process is *not* fun. None of it is for me until I can sit in a theater and see you laugh and cry at the result. One needs a truckload of passion to get through the process and at that moment my passion was elsewhere. I was writing the next book (still am). And I wanted desperately to finish it and take another shot at making life better for horses, and people. I loved what I was doing.

So we developed a financial model that would get us to the twins' graduation and allow me to continue to write. We would search for a new home in the southeastern quadrant of the country, not because I grew up there, but because most of it is gorgeous, green, temperate, and waaay cheaper than most other parts of the country. We would only consider areas and homes that would: 1) meet our financial model, which in a nutshell was that the mortgage, taxes and utilities could, in a pinch, all be paid by fixed income (see people, there is an advantage to being 70 :) and... 2) the horses could basically eat for free (instead of the extremely expensive California hay that we must buy all year long because there is no grass where we live; nor will there ever be because water and electricity are so expensive)... and preferably 3) the horses could drink for free as well... and that 4) if the economy does not recover and continues downhill we could even grow our own food if we had too ...and 5) have enough land that in a pinch other family members could come, build a cabin and make it through any financial crisis by going back to basics.

That was the plan and we vowed not to veer from it. I began on the internet and talked to a lot of friends and college mates, ultimately getting introduced to local realtors in east Texas, east Oklahoma, Arkansas, northern Georgia, Tennessee, North Carolina, Mississippi, and Virginia. Slowly we began to weave our way through hundreds of listings to the few that actually seemed to satisfy all of our criteria. Oh, I forgot to mention: the last criterion: access to fresh seafood and Starbucks :). We eliminated properties that even though they fit the model we just didn't like for one reason or another. Believe it or not, in the end, out of all the houses we looked at only two remained. One in Arkansas and one in middle Tennessee. And the one in Arkansas got knocked out because it sold before we could get over there to see it. It wasn't that close to a Starbucks anyway. So Kathleen got on a plane and flew to Nashville, met with the realtor and they headed for – are you ready? – Bell Buckle, Tennessee. Population 391. About six miles out of the town center, at the very dead end of a narrow gravel road, this is what she saw:

31 acres, most of it sloped-to-steep (which our herd is quite used to), a year-round spring that could be feeding an uncompleted pond right next to the pasture fence, and the price, taxes, and utilities fit the financial model perfectly. The house was nice and the 100-year-old barn looked like the model for a postcard. Since we'll never use it for stalling horses we plan to remove all the stalls, fix it up, let it be a run-in for the horses if they choose to during winter rains, and the rest of the time we'll use it for barn dances, music

camps, and horse workshops (while our herd mingles with at-
tendees).

What fun! Won't happen overnight because there's a lot of work to
do before any of that's possible, but it's something to look forward
to. Oh, and we're less than an hour from Nashville and Franklin
TN where Kathleen found two of the largest Whole Foods she had
ever seen – with fresh seafood – each just around the corner from
Starbucks :)

The down side of it all is that Kathleen will rent out here so
the twins can finish high school where they started. They're both
honor-role and AP students doing lots of extra curricula activities,
the teachers love them, and it would not be the best for their future
to make them start over in their junior year. So Kathleen and I will
be going back and forth for a year and a half. That will not be fun
but we know we're doing the right thing. For us. For the kids. For
the horses.

The horses and I will leave mid-September and move to Bell
Buckle. Kathleen and the kids will stay where we are now until the
house sells, then move into a rental house. Thanksgiving, Christmas, summers and other holidays will be in Tennessee.

It'll be another steep learning curve. Horses evolved for millions of years out in the Great Basin of the western United States. The high desert they call it. Our place in San Diego County was very similar terrain. Hard, dry, rocky. Middle Tennessee isn't. Not even close. So while I love the idea that they will have around-the-clock access to grass I worry about how their feet will fare on the softer, wetter terrain. But we'll figure it out. That's what makes life interesting (ask me again after the first winter).

For those who do not live in California, here are a few fun facts: Cost of registering our two cars and one pickup truck in CA: $1280 a year. In Tennessee: $108 a year. Property taxes on our California house: $9100 a year. The one in Bell Buckle less than $1000. Our average electric bill in CA: $600/month. In Tennessee around a $100/month. Water cost in Tennessee is 20% of the cost here in CA. Etc., etc.

Looking back, I'm still amazed we did it. The lessons learned? Don't wait. A complete and total makeover of your life is scary, but could be just what the doctor ordered. Whether it's about job, passion, expenses, or whatever. Humans have a tendency to get stuck. *I'm here so I must stay here. There's nothing I can do about it. It'll take too long or be too hard to figure out.* But it all starts by putting one foot in front of the other. Taking that first step. We started by calling one friend, who connected us up with one realtor. We looked at hundreds of houses. Only two fit the model. And one of those was terrific. It worked. Look at those huge looming tasks as a process. Lay the first brick. Shake off the human hunger for instant gratification. Just do it.

20

A STANDING OVATION
FOR MOUSE

Last night was an emotional ride. With only two weeks remaining before the movers were scheduled to come, Benji and I had to travel to Des Moines to speak at The Animal Rescue League of Iowa's annual fund raiser: The Mane Event. At the end of the presentation I attempted to demonstrate to the donors and supporters of the ARL how important they are to the League's work of saving animals; how their support is actually making a difference. Not only saving but changing lives… of people (mine and Kathleen's) as well as animals. Our Mouse was the subject.

Two years ago, seven-month-old Mouse was among 14 horses rescued by the ARL from horrendous, deplorable conditions near Des Moines. Mouse was among four chosen to make a trip to Monty

Roberts' farm in Solvang, California to receive a bit of behavior modification so they would all be more adoptable. Mouse was a growing baby and she was skin and bones, with awful feet, matted mane and tail, vacant eyes... and she was terrified of humans.

The first time she was maneuvered into the trailer-loading pen she jumped the fence. It ultimately took six big men to wrestle her into the trailer for the trip west. Two days after she arrived Monty took Mouse into a small – but very tall – corral and in thirty minutes was using her as a podium.

I was among a platform full of students watching and I was quietly falling in love. My stepson Dylan and I had driven up to Solvang with two of our horses at Monty's request to monitor the week-long seminar he was teaching. I snapped a cell-phone photo of Mouse and sent it off to Kathleen.

"We don't need another horse!" she responded. The tone was emphatic, finality dripping from every word.

"But, Sweetie…" I sniveled into the phone, "this one's had so many problems. She needs us."

"We already have six horses."

"But we don't have a baby.

"She's a baby???"

There was a long moment of silence.

"Wipe that smile off your face," she said.

Kathleen knows me too well. I zoomed in on Mouse's feet and snapped another picture and sent it quickly. She said it's the last time I will ever leave home with only two horses in a three-horse trailer. And I was off to call Carol Griglione at the ARL.

I relayed all this to the supporters of The Animal Rescue League last night… and then showed them a video entitled: *Mouse – Two Years Later* – all made possible by their support. The ovation was overwhelming. "You are part of a love story involving many," I said. "Without you, the supporters of the ARL, this would've never happened to Mouse… or to me and Kathleen… or to the hundreds and hundreds of other animals rescued and adopted out by the amazing folks at the Animal Rescue League. I thank you so very much."

It was a splendid evening indeed. Many thanks Carol, Dan, Tom, Julie and everyone in Des Moines

To watch the video go to the website or the blog and click *Video: Mouse –2 Years Later* in the right-hand column.

21

REFLECTIONS

We fed the herd for the last time on their dusty rocky hillside this morning. Kathleen and I had to work at holding ourselves together. She filmed it all because we realized that we had never recorded the entire procedure before and this would be the last opportunity. Seems appropriate somehow. The final California feed. The gang seemed to know something was afoot, especially when I walked out with all five of their tubs. Noelle is the big question mark, moving her into the shuttle trailer that will take her down the hill to the big travel trailer (which cannot get up our steep driveway). It will be an interesting test of keeping our adrenaline at rock bottom, and taking the time that it takes. Please say a prayer.

This is all suddenly very scary. We're actually going to do this. The first set of movers came on Friday. Today the horse transport comes. Tomorrow the tractor and the Gator leave. The next night is the world premiere of my youngest son's directing debut (*Love Happens*). The following morning Kathleen, Benji and I climb on a plane and fly into Nashville, and the next day the horses arrive in Bell Buckle. Being so wrapped up in the details of the process has helped me push aside how scary it all really is.

As I look back on this time from a distance of just over a year I'm still amazed that we actually made it happen. It's one thing if you have no choice, like the company you work for is transferring you, or you feel you must be closer to family, but to make this grand plan to move to a strange place where you don't know a soul simply because you think it's the right thing to do… like I said, I'm still amazed. Obviously we had little time for blogs because this chapter is the consolidation of three separate posts that when all bunched together is still shorter than any entry since the blog began.

Later that night this was posted:

It took 4 hours to load Noelle into the shuttle trailer! About thirty seconds to get her from the shuttle into the big transport (more spacious!). Kathleen filmed it all. A mini-series! And several very tired folks. One very close call. Thanks so much Dani, Gail, Dar, Mary Ann, and Julio… and, of course my sweetie. Now the herd is headed for Tennessee. Noelle and Cash will sleep well tonight. As will we.

Shame on me. One should never write a tease like *One very close call* and then walk away. To Noelle's credit, none of it was really her fault. And once again there were an abundance of good lessons learned. Like horses prefer lots of space to a little space.

Duh.

But our brains – and plans – got warped when, in the beginning, we couldn't even get Noelle close to the trailer, to sniff it out, or take a bite of her favorite hay. She simply would not get near it and as her adrenaline rose we were seriously afraid she might try to jump the fence or run over somebody. Part of her issue was just plain mustang fear, but part of it was also that the steep nature of the property and the many twists and turns in the driveway made the best loading configuration way short of good. Noelle had to work up an incline to get into the trailer which itself was on an uphill slant.

My brilliant idea was to bring Cash over and put him in the forward half of this small borrowed stock trailer. To demonstrate to Noelle that it was safe. And that plan worked, up to a point. Cash did draw her to the trailer and she seemed to get reasonably comfortable with it. That's the point when I should've taken Cash out and opened the divider in the trailer. But so pleased were we with it all seemingly going so well that no such thoughts occurred to us. Or at least to me. I started moving the hay farther and farther back into the trailer, closer to the center divider. And sure enough, to everyone's surprise, Noelle finally climbed in.

If it had been our trailer, the one she had come from Reno in, the one she at least was familiar with, the one with much more space even with a horse in the forward compartment, this entry might've worked. But our trailer was already in Tennessee, having made the trip filled to the roof with packed boxes.

Noelle was in the trailer, standing nose to rail with the center divider, when Dani, our trimmer, took her cue and began swinging the door shut. She couldn't see and didn't realize that Noelle's butt was still poking out a bit. When door met butt there was no way for Noelle to go forward so she freaked out and threw all her weight backwards against the door, slamming it open and knocking Dani to the ground. Noelle wheeled around and headed for her stall with Dani sprawled on the ground dead center in her path. But instantly and with the grace of a ballet dancer she sidestepped to intentionally miss Dani, and amazingly all was well. Dani had a backside bruise but was otherwise none the worse for wear. Thank God. And she insisted that she continue to man the trailer door. We added Julio to assist.

None of that would've happened if Cash had been removed and the divider had been opened. Noelle would've had room to move forward.

Which is exactly what happened an hour-and-a-half later when she, again, went in on her own. This time, she had the whole trailer to herself so she continued all the way to the front, then turned around, head facing the door, and just relaxed, sort of, as the door swung shut. Much better. Much safer.

The next day we got a call from Gail, the transport owner, saying all were travelling nicely and Noelle had eaten from a bucket in hand that morning. Not without a shiver, but she did do it. Good girl.

Two days later Kathleen, Benji and I were on the ground in Tennessee waiting for the arrival of our furniture and horses.

It took over six months of searching, planning, and execution to bring all this together but it seemed like it happened overnight. Like one of those impulsive decisions made in an instant that brings on the shivers.

That, we discovered, is what the big front porch overlooking the pasture is for. Shiver removal. And it truly works.

22

THE HORSES HAVE LANDED

Our timing was perfect. The move from dry rocky southern California landed us right in the middle of record-setting rainfall. Seven inches the day the horses came in. And it's been raining for days prior to their arrival. Gail Murphy's Personalized Equine Transportation Service has a reputation for never being late, but on this day they were. The rains slowed them to a crawl causing them to arrive after dark. Which is when we learned that the turn onto our road was too tight for their rig to make. We had to shuttle the horses off the transport trailer onto our 3-horse trailer which had to be pulled by a generous new neighbor with his 4-wheel drive tractor because my truck would've been mud-bound for sure.

Noelle went into a paddock in front of the barn and the hillside herd got the paddock behind the barn for the night. We didn't think it wise to turn them out on an unfamiliar *muddy* hillside at night. *Is that another one of those human things like blankets in the snow :).* They hadn't been out of the trailer for ten minutes when every one of them began to wallow in the mud like little pigs.

And through it all I could only think about what all this wet and mud might do to their beautiful, dry, rock-solid hooves.

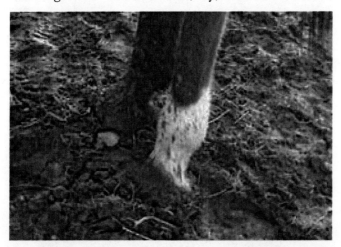

Everyone was in fine (however muddy) shape the next morning. Noelle was thoroughly enjoying being just over the fence from the herd and everybody seemed quite relaxed for being in such a strange place after travelling more than 2000 miles across the country.

We checked the footing on the smaller of the two pastures, the one closest to the house, and decided to open the gate let 'em have at it. It was definitely an YeeeHaaww moment, like so many of you have asked about and predicted. Cash trotted through of the gate and without ever looking back broke into a full run up the hill and off

toward the house. Within moments the other four were right behind him. Running, romping, and kicking up their heels! And
Kathleen got it all on video (no stills unfortunately. She still only
has two hands). *Hopefully by time this book is published I'll have the
footage edited and up on the website.* It was something to see. Meanwhile poor Noelle could only hang by the fence and pace and holler
at them.

When the herd finally calmed down their joy dissolved into disbe-
lief . There was grass everywhere they looked! I'm pretty sure that
four of the five had lived their entire lives in the west and had never
seen anything like this. They were fun to watch, but it was also
more than a little bit scary. We had received numerous warnings
that horses could not come here from the deserts of southern California and be out 24/7 on the very "rich grasses of middle Tennessee."

Too much sugar in this grass, we were told. Some had called the area "Founder Valley." I was worried about it to be sure, but I had done enough study of horses in the wild to feel that something was amiss with that logic. It's more complex than just sugar in grass. All grass everywhere in the world generates sugar. Can soil alone cause an over abundance? And how much does lots and lots of movement play into digestion and metabolism? Can supplements balance other things that if left unbalanced would be bad for the horse? And how much can stress from confinement and human-adjusted lifestyle play into metabolism imbalances. I didn't know, but I was already researching to find out. One of the points of moving here was to be able to truly let the horses live like horses. Like they were genetically evolved to live. And I wouldn't give that up without knowledge certain.

I was reminded of a piece I had read in a book about the San Diego Zoo's adoption of two gorilla's they wanted to mate. They fed the exact same leaves the gorillas had been eating in the wild, or so they thought. But the gorillas did not do well and did not mate. After a bunch of further research they finally discovered that when they were washing the leaves (so they'd be nice and clean) they were removing all the little bugs and microscopic life that were actually adding approximately 15% animal protein to the gorilla diets. They quit washing the leaves and the gorillas got better immediately, and mated.

I am now on a mission to "find the bugs" so to speak. To discover why horses in the wild can spend their entire spring and summer on beautiful rich-looking meadows and do just fine, but horses (or at least *some* horses) in middle Tennessee can't. I'll keep you posted.

There is so much mud in Noelle's paddock that I finally let her go out into the larger pasture if she chose to do so... which she did straightaway. I hoped and prayed that I could get her back at feeding times. But did I worry about it? Of course I did. I'm me. And it was, like most of the time, worry without foundation. She was back for every feeding. She looked rather majestic this afternoon perched up on the hill. It's obvious that I've come to completely depend on Kathleen for photo taking because it never occurred to me to pull out my cell phone until I was back at the house.

For the last couple of days Mouse has been favoring her right rear leg. She was the most recalcitrant of the six coming out. Being so young she has never been able to stand still for very long without getting antsy. Still I suspected she had pulled something skiing around on the hillside. It's been a mess. But today our new vet was out and found a small trauma at the hairline of her right rear hoof, probably where she stepped on herself on the trip over. It'll be fine, he said.

It's amazing. Just when you think you have everything figured out God says, "Not so fast". We simply didn't count on moving into record rainfall. And tons of mud in the pre-selected morning and evening supplement feed zones. I'm excited that the washer and dryer are finally hooked up because I'm sliding through a pair of muddy jeans a day! God just wanted us to know after so much complaining about the dust in California that the opposite of dust has its downside as well :).

All the horses learned right away that water is now from a pond instead of a big metal tub. Skeeter immediately got into the swing and went almost up to his knees. Even Cash who especially hates mud drinks his fill. I wonder how long it'll be before Mouse leaps in belly first?

Rains notwithstanding, I think we're all basically well if we can just get dried out a bit. The rains quit just long enough for the lawn to be mowed yesterday, but they were back again today. I wonder how long this will last?

I found out later that I shouldn't have asked. It turned out to be the wettest fall on record in middle Tennessee. We had over 26 inches during our first six weeks.

23

A DAY OF SUNSHINE

Finally, after 12 straight days without sun we had a picture perfect morning. This photo was taken high up on the hill above our home. Everybody was present except Mariah. I completely lost track of time, somewhat dazzled by it all, and just sat quietly breathing in the view. And watching the horses.

I told Kathleen that this experience in moving to Tennessee was like my former sailing days. When it was bad it was usually really bad, but when it was good it was glorious. Highs and lows. That's what life is made of :). I guess that's why I never cared for California. It's pretty much always the same. Today in middle Tennessee it was (finally) sunny and incredible.

Moments like this do tend to make it all worthwhile.

24

IT WAS THE BEST OF TIMES
IT WAS THE WORST OF TIMES

I ate dinner on the front porch tonight. Broiled salmon and spinach sautéed in olive oil and garlic while listening to the rain. What Kathleen and I call an Asheville rain, in honor of what was perhaps her first understanding (for a California girl) of how nice a rain can be. We were attending a Celtic music festival in Asheville. It was a Sunday morning and we were eating brunch at a little restaurant in an old house near the Biltmore Estate. No wind. No storm. Just a moderate rain falling straight down. Warm temps. Sweet sounds. There were two tables outside on the front porch and we had one of them. A three-hour brunch. At one point Kathleen reached across the table and squeezed my hand and said, "At last I understand why you like rain so much."

That was then. This is now. What I'm experiencing at the moment would be really sweet were it not for the fact that my Sweetie is in California and I'm in Tennessee... and this rain is expected to add at least two inches to the 24+ we've had since we brought the horses here barely four weeks ago. This is October. Which I'm told is by record supposed to be the driest month of the year in middle Tennessee. And we have six horses out there in the darkness at least five of which have never seen this much rain in an entire year in southern California.

This extreme life change brings out the worries. Especially the ominous warnings we've had about horses being out 24/7 on the "rich grasses" of middle Tennessee. The research is underway and I *will* get to the bottom of that issue. But rain rot could be a problem. Ever heard of that? I hadn't. Rain rot is a condition – especially with horses not used to rain - that is caused when the undercoat does not have time to dry between rains. Crusty lesions form that are not serious unless there's never time to dry out… which has definitely been the case here. So that became a new worry on the list when crusty lesions began to pop up. You think you've planned for everything in the "driest month of the year" but God says *not so fast.*

Our new vet, Dr. Bobby West, is very bright and very knowledgeable of local issues and he says these crusties are not rain rot. They're caused by skin allergies from exposure to foliage the horses have never seen before. It could take 18-24 months for the guys on the hill to adjust. Mouse worried me with a swollen left hind that turned out to be an allergic reaction to a thorny weed. Worry, worry, worry. One has to wonder: Was it better in Asheville? No horses. Just a lovely rainy morning brunch. Sweet happy faces.

No. I've learned over the years that there is no perfect answer. Life is not a spectator sport. Life is not a perfect sport. But it is one worth living. So do it. Take the chances that can stir your life and embrace the changes they bring. Some, unquestionably, won't be fun. Others will be spectacular.

Like salmon and sautéed spinach on the front porch with an Asheville rain falling.

25

FINDING THE BUGS
STEP ONE

Wild horses don't founder on grass. Some domestic horses do. And I was determined to find out why. Like the earlier story of the two gorillas at the San Diego Zoo, there had to be answers. And the logical place to begin is out there where there is no human intervention. Where no one is washing the bugs off the leaves. Out there in the wild.

During our tele-workshop on *Why Barefoot* we drifted into the role that diet and nutrition play in the barefoot lifestyle (huge!) and there was much talk about Spring grasses, high sugar content, etc. After the workshop I was glancing over some of the questions from participants, and Ginger Kathren's PBS series of "Cloud" documentaries that follow one particular wild herd in Montana's Pryor Mountains came to mind. Every Spring, once the snow has melted enough, the wild horses head for a beautiful huge meadow on top of the mountain, staying there for most of the Spring, Summer, and early Fall. So I asked Eddie Drabek (natural hoof specialist and one of our workshop guests): "What's the difference? If Spring grasses are not supposed to be good for horses, then how do these mustangs get by. How do they deal with it. To our knowledge none of them have ever foundered because of the Spring/Summer grasses."

Eddie's answer was, I thought, brilliant. Loaded with super information, analysis, and a road map of questions for further research. It follows below. The underlines are mine.

Joe – In the wild the grasses are native grasses…and unstressed grasses. Of course I realize there are times of drought but typically grasses left in their natural state handle such things quite well. Grasses going through the natural cycle they are meant to go through. <u>Never mown down</u> (other than naturally grazed over time each year), <u>not overwatered, with no pesticides or chemical fertilizer,</u> and not encouraged to grow in a season they aren't meant to. Also, th<u>e wild horse meadow is not just one sort of rich lush "genetically improved" grass,</u> like all Orchard, or what not. It's a mix. The horses have CHOICE. I wonder, is the wild area very lush and thick or is it still for the most part (compared to many domestic pastures) fairly scattered grasses which would help slow grazing and create more browsing…which helps the digestive system handle things more efficiently.

Some native species of the grasses may be richer, some not. Do these "non-rich" grasses with lower starches/sugars perhaps cut or dilute the sugar of the richer grasses?

It's also longer blade grasses…unstressed grass….For instance every spring I see changes in my horses hooves…some rings, maybe lose a little concavity here and there. Not enough to make them sore. I keep my two founder-prone ponies drylotted or they would show more damage. Most would never notice, but the changes are there. Because our grass pretty much stays stressed. We have nothing but bright green little nubs of "candy grass" as I call it, since the pasture is overgrazed…I have too many horses on too small of acreage, so not much I can do other than keep them penned up the majority of the time which I hate doing of course.

I trim for a few clients who have large 40-50 acre pastures, with just 4-5 horses and tall healthy grass. A small few will show some changes and yes, I've had some founder cases (being fed hi-sugar grain was the cause in my opinion) but the majority have no problems. Because the grasses are tall, healthy, and non-stressed, thus lower starch/sugar. And typically on larger acreage there are a lot of native grasses, not all one type as in small paddocks.

Mustangs start to drop weight in the fall typically, after getting a great weight during spring/summer. This is as nature intended. They get lean after a hard winter with less forage, and what forage is there is dry and dormant. Then spring hits and the horses are more able to handle spring grasses because they *need* it coming out of winter. Many of the mares are in final stages of pregnancy, they definitely need it to get ready for baby. If they started out being fat and chunky after winter and were put on the spring grass this might be a much different scenario.

Domestic horses don't *need* the rich grasses to "come out of winter" the way a wild horse does, which is why it causes them issues. We keep them fed and fat through winter...panic if they do drop some weight. What's worse...we still tend to feed them the same exact amount of grain/feed, alfalfa, etc. we were feeding through winter, PLUS now they are getting grass...I tell people all the time, if they are getting a lot of grass, you HAVE to cut back on everything else (really they probably need nothing else). But people still feed...asking them to quit feeding pellets or grain I've found is like asking them to give away their first born child, they look at you like you are plum crazy.

Also, there's movement in the wild. The mustangs are getting a lot of movement. A lot! This helps I am certain.... They aren't being confined, have good firm ground. They aren't living on soft shaving or arena sand part of their day, aren't getting grains, sweet feeds, or alfalfa, etc.

Domestic horses, <u>particularly those that are stalled during part of the night/day, tend to gorge when let out on pasture</u>, even when it's baking hot. Their inner clocks are amazing...they know when it's about time for them to be caught up and taken back to their pen or stall and they'll begin to "gorge" when they know that time is running out.

From summer heat and from less rain, grasses start drying out a bit by mid summer... By end of summer, when the grasses are probably getting to the point of possibly being overgrazed if this herd is staying fairly localized, it's time for the grass to get that final "Fall Boost" where they get a little spring like for a short period (which is beneficial/natural for the Wild Horses and other grazing wild life to help prepare for winter and get a few extra pounds on). Then the grass starts dying off/going dormant for winter...right when the horses start heading down the mountain...

I would LOVE to study this; wish someone would send in grasses and see how they differ from grasses in the typical domestic pasture situation...both spring grass and summer grass. See if there is even slight ripples in the hooves ever in some of the horses. See if their grazing habits change much from spring to summer. Nothing has changed more in natural hoof care than the diet info. The trim is the same, diet thoughts change each week it seems. For instance now many are questioning Soy and this is what they hoped would be a safer alternative to alfala/corn based feeds. It is definitely something I wish more people would research...quit researching in the labs of Purina and Nutrena, and research extensively in the wild habitats...what we could learn would be fantastic. – Eddie

I discovered later that some of this research had already been done. More on that in the next report on Finding the Bugs. Meanwhile Eddie's email really got my logic wheels spinning. Of course the wild horse meadows differ from a man-made pasture. So the obvious questions are how are they different, and why does that difference make a difference with the horses? Stay tuned.

26

"MAYBE HE TAUGHT YOU SOMETHING EXTRAORDINARY"

Last night I finally bit the bullet and began to read the huge stack of cards and letters sent to Kathleen and me after Malachi's death. I had put it off time and time again. I considered not packing them when we approached the move to Tennessee. I knew they were all full of love and compassion, but I still couldn't open the first one.

Finally, after staring at the pile for days as I packed up my study, I tossed them in a box and when that box was later unpacked I piled them all onto the table behind my desk, there to confront me everyday until eventually I pulled out the letter opener. As you have no doubt heard me say: *we have managed all this by focusing forward, not backward.* So I was still reluctant.

A couple of weeks ago Kathleen was wandering through the hundreds of pictures she had taken of Malachi and sent me one I had never seen. The one on the previous page. It broke my heart. I cried it seems for hours. So the piles of cards and letters just sat, and sat, for more than four weeks.

Until last night.

I was up way too late. But I read every one. Every word. At one point over the last several months I vowed to answer every one personally but last night I changed my mind and ask your forgiveness. I just can't. But I thank you each and every one for all the beautiful words of love and hope and care and concern. The chapter headline above is but an example of how each message attempted to buoy us, to help us get through it. To refill the vacuum. The entire line read: *Maybe he taught you something quite extraordinary that will help the lives of other horses in the future."*

Nothing can refill the vacuum, of course, but we so appreciate all the efforts.

I was in the pasture all day today running electric fence. It was only the second day since we arrived in Tennessee with sunshine, and there wasn't a cloud in the sky. Cold, still muddy, but beautiful. I had a lot of help from the herd. Unfortunately Kathleen was in California and wasn't here to document it. At one point the herd wandered off to the far end of the larger pasture and I glanced over at Noelle in the paddock behind the barn, and the following picture of Malachi stepping onto his platform flashed through my conscientiousness:

Because here's what I saw:

Sorry for the quality. It was taken with my old phone. Noelle is standing on a concrete pad, about a foot off the ground, behind our new 100-year-old barn. She has never – to my knowledge – been on that platform. She still walks huge circles around anything new or never seen before. Right or wrong, I believe what she saw Malachi do over and over convinced her that such was okay, it could be trusted. Actually Malachi's little platform is just out of frame to the left and I wished that it had been out there where she's standing…

wondering if she would be on that as well… for what she appeared
to be doing was to stand taller in an attempt to see the herd which
had wondered off over a hill toward the far end of the larger pasture.

As I stood there watching her, cell camera in hand, I also
thought about this photo:

This one was taken just a couple of weeks after Malachi's death.
One of Noelle's first times in Malachi's playpen. She left Kathleen
and me and the alfalfa sprinkled at our feet and walked over to sniff
around her baby's platform, which by his third month he would
often climb upon completely on his own and hang his head over
into Noelle's (open) stall, surely saying *Look at me mom. I'm a big
boy* now.

We've all learned from him haven't we Noelle?

Kathleen and I Skype every night. In California we would sit
around the dinner table long after the meal was finished and just
talk. About stuff. Often even the kids would hang and join the conversation. We miss that and I'm not sure we could last through this
time of being apart without Skype. Last night I tried to read to her
from some of the cards and letters, but she wouldn't listen, still not

ready. I wasn't either when I finally read them, but I did make it through, and I thank you so very much. It's the stuff of life. Which is definitely better than any alternative.

I love you guys.

27

AUTUMN ROSES

Sometimes I have to haul off and slap myself.

Seriously.

Something to force the brain to stop racing around like a crazed maniac and take a deep breath. To pause and smell the roses. Or at least *look* at them. How many times in my life have I closed my eyes and dreamed of the above picture? Horses on a beautiful hillside pasture grazing lazily beneath a spectacular swath of brilliant fall colors. And here it is. Part of our life. And I'm fretting about how far behind I am and how much I have to do.

But I'm getting better, especially on days like this.

It's hard to believe that we've been here almost two months. Yet, sometimes it seems like two years. Those who have followed our move from southern California to middle Tennessee know it's been filled with (shall we say) interesting challenges. Seven inches of rain on the day our ultra-dry southern California horses arrived, followed by twenty-five additional inches over the next six weeks. Mud so thick and gooey that it sucked my boot right off my foot was everywhere the horses wanted to be. They never seemed to dry out. People were still preaching at me from every direction that there's no way our desert horses could or would survive the rich Tennessee grasses if they were out 24/7.

Did that bother me? I'll say. My sermons all revolve around giving the horses a life that's as close to what it would be in the wild as circumstances allow. *Give them plenty of choices and they will make the right decisions for themselves.* And as Rick Lamb said in a recent blog, it was time to walk the talk. To set 'em up for natural success and get out of the way. Our pastures are mixed grasses, unfertilized for at least eight years and thus not "rich" (chemical fertilizer is terrible for horses). We have lots of weeds, brambles, trees, and scrubs. And lots of movement because the spring fed pond is on one end of the 31 acres and their favorite munching is on the other end.

But within the first week, three of the herd had hive-like allergic reactions and I panicked. They evolved into crusty bumps which the vet tech thought was rain rot. The vet said no. He felt sure it was all part of a reaction to some strange weed they had never encountered before. *A little antihistamine and a good frost and they'll be fine*, he said. And sure enough, they were. Mouse's left hind ankle swelled up like a balloon and she was limping. I feared the worst. Dr. West felt like she had encountered a certain thorny weed and the toxins in the thorns had caused a vascular swelling. He took a blood sample for confirmation and gave her a shot. That afternoon she was galloping around the pasture with Cash. I love Dr. West!

The pasture-five had their first Tennessee hoof trim a week ago with our new trimmer Mark Taylor, a Pete Ramey believer, and was I ever impressed. Their feet looked super despite all the rain and mud and Tennessee grasses. Mark loved the pea gravel we had just installed at all the muddiest places including around the pond where the horses drink. And finally... two weeks of sun have done wonders for my spirits... and the horses' as well.

So stop with the worrying, Joe. Just stop it. Relax on that big front porch and soak up the spectacular view. And count your blessings.

28

NOELLE JOINS THE HERD

Kathleen was here last weekend and we decided it was time to let Noelle out with the herd. I was pretty certain, given the experience with Tennessee weather, that there was precious little progress going to be made with her during the winter so there was no need to keep her penned up any longer. And she needed movement. Plus her two paddocks controlled the barn which needed to be accessible to the entire herd as an optional run-in for winter weather.

"But how will you get her isolated again to feed her supplements or work with her," Kathleen asked.

"It's called trial and error horsemanship," I said. "Gotta trust yourself to be able to figure it out."

Brilliantly said, I thought, but I was secretly afraid that I might never see her again. I opened the gate, and waited.

Kathleen had the still camera and I was shooting video. Noelle just stood there for the longest time gazing at the open gate before she finally started to move. None of which was going unnoticed amongst the herd.

Finally she started out. The video of what happened next is amazing (and someday will make it to the website). There were definitely fisticuffs as Noelle sought to establish her dominance. The "B" word was blurted more than once by both of us and will have to be eliminated from the soundtrack. Her first target was Mariah.

She walked right up to her and said *Move!* Mariah pined her ears and said *I'm very happy where I am thank you very much. Buzz off!* The mustang's next move happened so fast that Kathleen missed the picture. Noelle did a half spin and fired a kick at Mariah in the chest. All in one lightning fast move! The photo below is probably less than a second later. Just amazing how fast she was. Thank goodness Kathleen kept shooting. My video camera was still rolling but I was frozen with my mouth hanging open.

Noelle nailed her good.

But Mariah came right back at her. *So that's the game, is it?* And Kathleen's timing was perfect this time.

Make my day!

I missed what was said next, but the kick fest was suddenly over and two minutes later they were side-by-side munching grass and Noelle was the new herd leader.

Cash is non-violent. He watched the goings-on for a bit then wandered off well away from it all, ceding his crown without a blink or an encounter. *I'll have nothing to do with such uncivilized behavior.* The aggravation is simply not worth it to him. Back when Scribbles

was the herd leader he was pretty much of a jerk to everyone, constantly reminding each herd member: *I am da boss and don't you forget it!* Cash just stayed out of his way. When Scribbles left the herd,
Cash ascended slowly to the throne, very quietly, very politely. And
there he's been until now. I suspect that he'll be back in time. But
he'll do it *his* way. He and Noelle hang out a lot together.

Then three-year-old Mouse tried to nurse on Noelle. Which was
very strange and a bit too much for her. She ended it firing a kick at
Mouse. All in all Noelle kicked or kicked *at* everybody but Cash
and Pocket, who pretty much just stayed away, wanting no part of
such conduct.

The most interesting part of it all, at least to me, is that from
those moments on there have been no issues from Noelle. She's as
calm and peaceful with her leadership as Cash was. Sometimes
nothing more than a tiny flick of her head. The only one she ever
gets a little testy with is Mouse, who usually deserves it. I get a little
testy with Mouse myself on occasion. But, unlike Scribbles, Noelle
always asks politely first, then ramps up as necessary.

Kathleen will tell you that I'm terrific at manufacturing worries when there's no need whatsoever. The day Noelle went into the
herd I would not leave the scene until she had successfully discov-

ered her source of water. She had never had access to the smaller
pasture before and the pond is at the far end. I actually worried that
she wouldn't find it. Of course she was quietly drinking less than an
hour later.

Again, from the distance of a year and a half, it seems funny to
me that I was so freaked out during those first few weeks. And it
just reemphasizes how much we humans seem determined to get in
the way. To *make* the horses live the way *we* feel is best instead of
the way *they* feel is best. During all the rain and mud I was actually
wishing for some dry stalls with hard floors. Would I have used
them? I hope not. Noelle had the barn to herself at that time but
she was never in it except to walk through from one paddock to the
other. Never.

A bit of pea gravel (okay more than a bit) took care of the
worst of the muddy areas and now gives all the hooves many mas-
sages a day. From the moment Noelle joined the herd she has returned virtually every feeding time to exactly where she's been fed
since the day we arrived. And I believe she is now calmer with me
and more giving than ever. I had two hands on her face tonight,
face-to-face, rubbing both cheeks.. Trailing a hand down her back
as I passed by to bring the Gator in.

On another front, we built what I call "the chute" using portable Preifert corral panels. Now we can bring the Gator into the
pasture without leaving an escape hatch open to the herd. We drive
through the fence gate into the chute, close the fence gate and open
the chute gate. But it also turned out to be a handy way to isolate a
horse. They all know if they're invited in there'll be hay or of Safe
Starch waiting. So there are never any issues when someone needs a
shot, or when it's time to ride, which Kathleen and I actually did
last weekend when she was here. Not long and not far, but it was
fun. Kathleen's first time up in maybe six months. This is also
where Mark Taylor trims hooves. The floor of the chute is five-

inch thick pea gravel. When not being used, the gate and a panel are opened because they like to stand in the shade of the big tree. Photo below.

The entire herd now has access to the barn 24/7 except during supplement feeding times.

We pretty much follow the same menu as in California (it's on the website) with one big exception. Grass instead of hay (at least until December). At feeding times Noelle is isolated in the paddock from which this photo was taken. Cash, Pocket, and Mariah are fed in the paddock you see at the other end of the barn breezeway.

Uncle Skeeter and Mouse are fed in a shed on the right side of the barn. Once the grass is gone and we start supplementing with hay it will be scattered with the Gator over all the pasture areas to keep the gang moving most of the day; again, as we did in California.

So here we are with six happy healthy horses already very well adjusted and loving their natural life... as we continue to receive our life lessons from the herd while attempting to trust ourselves to figure it all out. Always being replenished, daily, hourly, by scenes like this.

29

CASH'S FIRST SNOWFALL

Actually it's probably the first snowfall ever for four of our six horses, three of our four dogs, and our kitty. Okay, okay, I know all you guys who live way on up there in the freezer are laughing your heads off at me calling this snow, but I was like a kid this morning (Kathleen is unfortunately in southern California and missing it all). It was exciting. Fun. And all the critters seemed to agree.

When I first looked out the window this morning I saw no horses. I was certain they must all be huddled inside the barn, bundled up together trying to stay warm, wondering what in the world had gone wrong with their world.

Not exactly.

They were all up in the far pasture munching away... frolicking and rolling in the snow! They came down covered in it, with icicles hanging off their ears, manes, and forelocks. Mariah executed a perfect slide stop when she realized she was going so fast she was going to run into the gate. Cash and Mouse were acting like kids (Mouse is, but Cash isn't).

Even the sedate old man Skeeter was kicking up his heels and tossing his head.

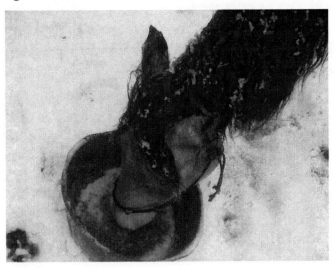

It was such a beautiful morning. I was well-bundled so only my toes got cold and that of course made me worry about *their* toes. How come it is that no matter how much we know we cannot help but project our human-ness onto our horses. They have the barn if they need it but I still have to whap myself to keep from forcing it on them. Or wanting to. But now Rick Lamb is watching over us with his blog statement: *Walk the talk!* Which means set 'em up for success and get the heck outta the way.

Ahhh. Cappuccino and snow. Nice. *I was ignoring what it might mean. It was one of the earliest snows ever in this part of Tennessee.*

30

WORDS THAT MADE MY DAY

A day doesn't pass that we don't receive several beautiful emails from folks who have read the book, the blog, a newsletter, the Facebook page, or been on the website and been moved by something we've said or done. These words are what make it all worthwhile. The juice that keeps our wheels turning and keeps us fired up about what we do. And keeps us ever focused on doing it better. The one below is very special however and left both Kathleen and me in a heap. But forever aware that this journey has been a worthwhile trip.

"I wanted to tell you how much your journey with Malachi meant to me, and to my Mom. I lost my Mom in August, the result of COPD, and debilitating arthritis. She was forced to live out her last year of life in an assisted living facility in Texas and when I would go visit her, I would take my computer, and we would look thru the newsletters, which I saved in my email for just that purpose. She really loved the photos of Malachi and Noelle, and was truly enchanted by your stories (as I was!). I did not have the heart to tell her when you lost Malachi, I just couldn't do it. She honestly had so little to look forward to, I just couldn't take that away from her. The last good visit I had with her, I told her that I had accidentally erased the newsletters, (a lie born of love, I assure you!) and we just reviewed the previous ones. They truly made her smile. I tell you this not to make you sad, but merely to let you know that your journey, as personal as it was for you and your family, was shared by many, and has left an indelible mark on me, and given me some very sweet, dear memories of my beloved mother. For that, I am eternally grateful.

As a side note, my sister-in-law (whom I'm buying another book for) has a daughter named Noelle." Shannon Terlop – Florida

Many years ago we did a picture without Benji called *The Double McGuffin.* It was about six teenagers at a private boarding school who stumbled upon a possible murder about to happen… but because they hadn't been – shall we say – the best behaved kids on campus, they were unable to convince the authorities that they were telling the truth. So… not content to sit back and watch this murder unfold, they were more or less forced to take matters into their own hands.

We cast this picture very carefully because even though we had a few well known character actors, the final result would rest squarely on the shoulders of these kids. It was a diverse group. A kid from Brooklyn, a young, very bright kid from Kansas, a pretty young photographer, a black musician from Florida, a good old boy from a ranch in Texas, and a first class absolute bookworm of a nerd.

In the final analysis, we did a great job casting. That is to say the kids we chose did a great job... all except one.

The kid from Texas. His name was Jeff. Before shooting was over I could have willingly let him be the murder victim. Turned out, even though his accent and manner were perfect, this kid couldn't read a line the same way twice. He couldn't walk and read a line at all. We had these long-winded, drawn-out complicated shots when everything and everybody would be perfect... except Jeff. I wanted to strangle him so many times I lost count.

Then... in editing... everything got worse. Much worse. You'd think that as the production wore on that I would have learned... and cut out those complicated shots... but noooo... Joe wanted perfection. I would be embarrassed at the language used in the editing room trying to keep Jeff from ruining an otherwise terrific movie. We would steal a word from this take... another word from another take... cutting them into yet a third take... which today, with digital editing, is not all that hard to do... but back then we were still working with these little bitty pieces of film and physically cutting them in with editing tape... it was a nightmare!

We were stealing cutaways from other parts of the film when none had been shot, just to get the camera off Jeff... basically doing whatever we had to do... "not quitting"... not letting Jeff turn this piece of silk into a sow's ear.

And you know what? In the final analysis, the kid looked great. Got smiles and laughs and great reviews. I was astounded.

I never saw or talked to Jeff after we left location... but I never forgot the misery he had caused us... or rather the misery our bad decision-making had caused us.

Twenty years later - in December of 1997 - when Carolyn, my first wife, died quite unexpectedly of sudden cardiac arrest... a letter arrived from Jeff. Understand that, at least for that moment in time back during production, I would've bet against him ever attending college and would've easily voted him least likely to ever accomplish anything worthwhile. His letter follows:

"Dear Joe:

I was saddened to read in the paper over the weekend of the death of Carolyn. I wanted to write and tell you how truly sorry I am for your loss.

"I never got to thank you two for the opportunity you provided me some twenty years ago to play a part in one of your films. It was not until many years after, that I realized that you and Carolyn provided me an opportunity that literally changed the course of my life. Along with beliefs instilled in me by my parents, the opportunity provided to me to be in your film gave me the strength and confidence to know that I could make decisions that would enable me to reach and attain levels that many people consider unreachable. For that I will be ever grateful.

Signed... Jeff Nicholson... Attorney at Law... Lubbock, Texas

Needless to say... I cried.

You just never know what you might be leaving in your wake. Or what might be happening out there in the world because of something you said, or did, or wrote. Those I hear about never fail to make my day, to cause me to stand a little taller and smile a little deeper, and thank my God for the opportunity He has given me to make a difference in this world.

31

LEARNING THE HARD WAY

The second snow arrived on January 2nd.

I was excited because Kathleen got to see her new home covered in white. White that would be virtually gone by the time we left for the airport the next day to return her to the twins in California. We were told it was supposed to be this way in middle Tennessee. Enough to be beautiful, not enough to hassle.

Not so with the snow that followed on the 8th. The first of 23 consecutive days of below freezing temperatures. We were told this never happens. The list of record-setting weather phenomena continued to grow.

Of course it wasn't long before the pond began to freeze over. Ooops.

I hadn't considered that. This never happens in middle Tennessee.

But the single source of water for the horses was definitely turning to ice. No question about it.

I was reasonably proud of myself actually. I would go out several times a day and chop around the edges of the pond so the horses would have no problem getting water. I would often watch them when they came to the pond and if a thin coating of ice had re-frozen, usually a single tap with a hoof would produce water and they would drink. As the number of days below freezing began to build into the double digits I would go out even more often to make sure the edges had water, or at worst that the ice was very thin, paying little attention to what was going on with the ice be-

yond the edges. It was getting thicker and thicker. Then one afternoon I left to run a couple of errands, returning about two hours
later.

The pond looked like an underwater bomb had exploded. This
photo was taken hours later. All that smooth ice you see was water
when I arrived on the scene. And the chunks were floating.

I panicked.

I jumped in the Gator and raced off for the barn. Five of the
six horses were standing just out front. Cash was unusually close to
Mariah, sort of rubbing on her butt. Sure enough as I hit the brakes
I could see a coating of ice on Mariah's back and she was shivering
uncontrollably. The temperature was in the mid 20s. And it was
windy. I ran up and looked into her eyes. Not happy, but seemingly
lucid. I scraped the ice off her back trying to act softly, calmly, but I
was freaking out inside, and couldn't decide what to do first. I
reached for the cell phone, then remembered it wouldn't work. The
cell is good for nothing but text at the house. Too far out in the
sticks and buried up in a hollow surrounded by hills. Beautiful but
really inconvenient at a time like this. It seems that not a day goes
by that we aren't slapped in the face by something we've never dealt

with before. That can be fun to figure out when life and death aren't involved. This was not fun. Then I noticed there was blood on her back left leg around the ankle. I looked closer, and she pulled it away. It didn't seem too serious but I wanted experienced hands on it. I blew in her nose, pushed Cash closer to her and raced back to the house as fast as the Gator would carry me to call the vet. He wasn't in. I spoke with Casey, his vet tech. She told me to get as many blankets as I could carry, get her out of the wind, and get the blankets on her. *Then see if you can examine her ankle.* Meanwhile she would find the doctor and text me the result of her phone conversation. She knows my cell phone's limitations.

Most of our blankets are still in California with Kathleen and the twins. There's only a limited supply in Tennessee. I found an unused furniture pad from the move. It wasn't the old quilted kind, but one made with a thick composite of fibers, sort of like a fabric press board. It turned out to be magic. I found two smaller lap blankets and couldn't find anything else so I snatched a comforter off of Allegra's bed, tossed them all into the Gator and raced back to the barn. I put a halter on Mariah and led her into the shed on the side of the barn. It's roofed and half of it is totally shielded from the wind. When I came at her with the furniture pad she wheeled and backed away. *At least she's moving well*, I thought. I balled it up as small as I could make it and let her sniff it, then began rubbing her face with the ball, then her neck, her back, slowly unfolding it until she was wearing it. Next came the two lap blankets, and finally the big heavy comforter. My hands pushed and pressed and rubbed and rubbed. Hard. Trying to soak up the water. She was offered her favorite Bermuda but she wouldn't eat. I kept thinking about the pond. It truly looked as if an explosion had gone off. I couldn't imagine what Mariah had been through. Well... yes I could, but I kept trying to shake it off. She must have been petrified.

Casey's text came in. *Dr West wants to know if you've been able to examine the foot.* I tried again and she pulled it away. *It's obviously sore but she's moving on it well because she won't let me close and I don't want to stress her by chasing the foot around right now. Can Dr. West come out?*

Yes. Tonight. But he has to finish where he is.

Any idea as to time.

No.

I couldn't leave because there was no way to safely secure the blankets. So I kept rubbing, and talking to her. She finally began to nibble the hay and slowly, seemingly ever so slowly, the shivering began to ease. The more she ate the more quickly the shivering subsided. It had stopped entirely by the time Dr. Bobby arrived. I told him what a wreck the pond was, guessing that, for whatever reason, she had stepped out onto the thicker ice, slipped and slid toward the middle of the pond trying to keep her balance, then fell and the impact of the fall broke the ice. Then she must've flailed her way back to the edge, breaking ice as she came.

He checked her leg while I rubbed her face. It was just a superficial scrape. Nothing internal. Nothing bad. He listened to all her body parts and examined her thoroughly. "She just might be the luckiest horse in Tennessee," he said. At one point he raised the blankets around her butt to show me the clouds of steam coming out. "Her heating engine is working well," he smiled.

I thanked God for a strong, healthy horse.

"You'll need some real horse blankets for the night. Ones that will stay on."

"I don't have any." A once proud statement.

He called Casey. She would lend me two. I should sandwich a couple of the ones she was wearing between the real ones. They shouldn't come off until she was totally dry and the sun was out, which was, in fact, supposed to shine the next day before the snow started again that night. When I re-organized the blankets I noticed that the furniture pad, which was next to her body, was very wet on the bottom, but not wet on the top, and the lap blankets above it were soaked. That's why I called it magic. It was wicking the water away from her body and into the blankets above. After putting on the first real horse blanket, which seemed to take hours because I had never strapped one on before, I inverted the furniture pad, dry side down, then added the second big thick horse blanket. The furniture pad is from UHaul and is very inexpensive, just in case you want to have one handy.

I thanked God for her warmth. For Dr. Bobby. For Casey, and her blankets. And for the fact that the pond was only five feet deep in the middle. Once I had considered digging it deeper.

Being able to plant her rear feet on the bottom is what gave Mariah the traction to use her front feet to break ice and work her way back to the edge of the pond and onto hard ground. I have since heard some horror stories about similar situations that didn't end as well.

I checked on Mariah around midnight. She was doing fine. Chomping away on her huge tub of hay.

On the way back to the house I closed off the entire pasture to keep everyone away from the pond. Off limits to all horses. All gates closed.

Their water source became a "freeze-proof" spigot in the barn with a tub nuzzled right up to next to it (couldn't use a hose for obvious reasons). The next morning, of course, the water in the tub was topped with two inches of ice so it was off to the local Co-Op to find a heating element. I purchased their last one. The electric cord had to be run through a PVC pipe to keep Mouse's hyper-curious teeth from eating through it.

For someone with no contractor skills whatsoever this tiny task was like building a house :) But, finally, just as the snow started again, I got it finished and it all seemed to work as advertised.

Until the 18th day of below freezing temps.

When the freeze-proof spigot froze.

I think the low was 12 degrees that night. Since then I've been filling three large tubs of water in the kitchen, then hauling them down to the barn in the Gator. Three to four times a day. The last one usually around 10:30 pm. It's 17 degrees as I write this and 10:12 pm and here I go again to the barn.

Mariah was bone dry the morning after her splash down. The sun was out and by mid-morning she was naked once again and out with the herd. The photo below was taken later that afternoon as the snow returned.

Now for the confession. A mere hours before this all happened, Debbie Madras, a subscriber to our blog, had seen me breaking up the pond edge with a hoe in a blog photo and sent along this email: *Do NOT let your horses get out on the ice and fall through.* And I had politely said to myself: *No. I wouldn't. Of course. I have it all covered. We're good.*

My dad used to tell me that teaching and preaching notwith-standing, some of the best lessons in life come from the experience of being there and dealing with it. He was right of course. What my dad did not tell me is how serious the mistake could be of not making the forced effort to think it through in the first place, and planning for the worst. Although planning for the worst *every* time means living life always bundled up in fear. So it's pretty much always going to be shades of gray, never black and white. We all seem to prefer black and white. Unfortunately that's usually not where the right answers come from.

But it will be a long time before I forget what might have happened if I had climbed out of the truck and slipped in the back door of the house as I usually do. I would not have seen the pond. That thought sends a major shiver up my spine.

The snow went on for three days. The herd can be seen up the hill behind the trees. They spent virtually no time in the barn.

By the 14th of January the pond had de-iced and the next day the spigot in the barn finally broke loose and water flowed. I was one happy camper.

32

NOT DONE YET

Ever determined Ol' Man Winter clearly wanted to insure his place in history by presenting us with the 4th snow of the season on January 29th. The first reasonably serious one. As I write this there must be 4-5 inches of accumulation so far and more to come. For a while it was all predicted to be freezing rain and sleet, which the snow now seems to be turning to. It's exactly 32 degrees. I've been watching weather.com radar and we seem to be right on cusp between snow and the icy mix. I hope for the sake of the horses and power lines that the snow wins out.

The morning began like this:

Moments after this phone photo was taken snow began to fall. The reason I snapped it quickly with the phone was that I had never captured five of our six at the pond at the same time. They must've known what was coming and were stocking up. Two hours later it looked like this:

The dot on the right is Josie, our Australian Shepherd, who was enjoying it all immensely. As were the horses.

But as the day wore on the icy mix of rain and sleet began to take over and my worries ramped up. About tree limbs, power lines, and the horses. Snow is not a problem for the horse. But a soaking rain that freezes can wet their entire outer coat and undermine their ability to insulate and keep warm. Like when Mariah went in the pond. When I went down for the evening feed, everybody but Skeeter was under cover in the barn breezeway, so the plan Kathleen and I had discussed during our nightly Skype last evening was put into place. Mouse is the last in the herd pecking order but a pesky little kid who has always found a way to work her way into the barn if she wanted to be there. But Skeeter (number five in the pecking order) won't do that. He won't argue with anyone except Mouse. So I felt Mouse would be okay with the herd. But to ensure Skeeter a dry night if this rainy/icy mix continues he was locked in the side-shed of the barn with enough hay to last him till morning.

I don't like the idea of putting hay in the barn breezeway because I don't want to induce any fisticuffs over food... but tonight I broke the rule and lined one side of the breezeway, then put a bunch just outside the front and back entrances.

I went back down around 10:30 to check on them and put out more hay if necessary. The precipitation was still an icy mix. But only Mariah was in the barn breezeway. *Oh me. Where could they all be?* I worried. As I sloshed out into the back paddock, there they were, the missing four herd members, standing by Skeeter's gate, out in the rain and sleet, just to be near him. Just so he wouldn't be alone.

How very, very sweet, I thought. And I slid and skidded back up the driveway to bed.

33

AHHH... SUNSHINE AT LAST!

Four consecutive days of sun! The first time that's happened since we moved here last September (*This was posted on February 22ⁿᵈ*). Kathleen flew in Wednesday night and brought it all with her. There wasn't a cloud in the sky Thursday morning. Or Friday. Or Saturday. And just wispys on Sunday until she stepped back on the airplane. But it was wonderful to have her here... in the sunshine... and back behind the camera.

It's been a long six months with records set for the wettest Fall and worst Winter ever in middle Tennessee. Definitely a new and different world, full of adjustments for us and the horses.

And Mother Nature wasn't done with us yet. The pattern continued. We had the floodingest spring, the hottest summer, and, as I write this, the driest fall on recent record in these parts. I no longer even con-

sider asking the question: what next? But on this particular day in Feb-
ruary the sun was out and warming our souls.

We all celebrated a bit of faux Spring :) And Kathleen kept her shutter clicking.

Miss Mouse – loving it.

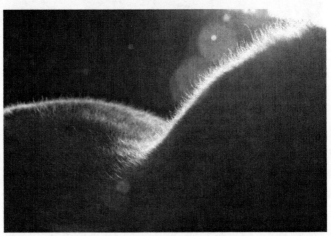

Skeeter too. Toasty rays.

I love this shot. It's beautiful in color. A day like this with Kathleen on this side of the country keeps me ever aware of how much I miss her photography and depend upon it for inspiration.

I'll just sit and soak for a while.

Miss Noelle and moi – just hangin'.

Of course three hours after Kathleen stepped onto the airplane it was raining again. I swear! Just unbelievable. I think neighbors would pay a fee for her return. I'm sure she can get more than lawyer rates for such a skill, especially *this* winter. One of our neighbors told her: *You can stay but your husband's tail has to leave.* They're all blaming me for the record setting weather from the first day we arrived with the horses. Problem is I'm blaming me too. Over the years we have crunched weather records filming in Oregon, Dallas,

Greece, Yuma, Arizona, and Utah. Sounds like a pattern to me. Scary.

But even with all the shattered records, the wet, the mud, the cold, and the ice, we are all doing okay. Adjustment to the new environment is taking hold. The horses' feet all look terrific and they appear to be getting a handle on the allergies. They love their expanded freedom with room to run. And they especially love this new-fangled grass that comes up out of the ground instead of off a truck. And they still come when I call, even with forage all around them.

I am, at last, beginning to look forward to all the lessons yet to learn, and all the joy that lies ahead.

PART THREE
THE JOURNEY CONTINUES

34

I Wish You Moments
That Calm Your Soul Like
This Does Mine

It's been too long. This is where Kathleen and I ate our first several dozen meals after the move last September. Breakfasts. Lunches. Dinners (or as they say here in middle Tennessee: Suppers). We would sit sometimes for an hour or more without a word. Just watching the herd. Listening to the symphony of the frogs at night. The birds. The crickets. *Smelling the roses.*

Locked up in the house over a seemingly endless winter, buried in work and warmth, the roses were fewer and further between. And easy to ignore. I often looked at it as a good thing because I was getting so much work done. Not bothered by those smelly old roses. But my spirit suffered. I only realized how much this morning. Out here at breakfast.

There was simply no choice.

Blood pressure dropped, breathing eased. And I glazed over for much of the morning. That snippet of time was worth all the 15-degree days, the rains, the snows, even the hand-lugging jugs of water to the barn after Mariah fell through the ice and shut down the pond and the "freeze-proof" spigot at the barn froze. Worth every bit of it. And when my Sweetie comes back next week life will once again be perfect. Thank you Lord.

35

FINDING THE BUGS
STEP TWO

As Spring began to flower and little green nubblets of grass began to come alive I was once again reminded by several that our horses shouldn't be out 24/7 on the "rich grasses of middle Tennessee." These warnings reignited a motivation to find answers to the puzzling question of why some domestic horses founder on grass. I call it puzzling because this simply doesn't happen in the wild. I reviewed Eddie Drabek's email (Chapter 25) and headed out to prove or disprove his hypothesis.

First I reviewed my list of Undeniable Truths developed for our tele-workshops on *Why Barefoot* and *Diet and Nutrition*. These are known and proven truths of science, not conjecture or opinion. The ones that apply to this issue are:

1. Science confirms that it would take a minimum of 5000 years – probably closer to 10,000 – to even begin to change the base genetics of *any* species. In other words, a few hundred years of selective breeding has no effect on base genetics whatsoever. Which means that the domestic horse and the horse in the wild are genetically exactly the same.

2. DNA sequencing was performed on bones of horses discovered in the Alaskan permafrost dating 12,000 to 28,000 years old and the results were compared to DNA sequencing from today's domestic horse. There was less than 1.2% difference between the two. Again confirming that the genetics of every horse on the planet are the same, and that

"every horse on the planet retains the ability to return successfully to the wild or feral state." Note the scientists use
the word: *successfully*. In other words, today's domestic
horse has the genetic ability to grow as perfect a foot and
take care of himself with no help from humans every bit as
well as those in the wild.

3.   The horse evolved for more than 50 million years in the
     Great Basin of the western United States. During those
     millions of years he developed genetics designed to *survive*
     and live in a specific lifestyle in a specific manner. To eat
     in a specific way. To move a specific amount. To socialize
     in a way that provides for a specific need. The domestic
     horse of today retains those genetics which program his
     lifestyle to:

     a.   Move a minimum of ten to thirty miles every day
          of his life in search of food, water, and staying
          ahead of predators. Living without this movement
          causes physical and mental stress to the horse.

     b.   Eat tiny bits of forage – mostly *grass* forage - little
          bits at a time, virtually around the clock; a mini-
          mum of 16-18 hours a day, or more. Their tum-
          mies are tiny and not meant to eat two or three
          large meals a day, and their hindgut *requires* the
          constant passage of grass forage through it in or-
          der to perform and digest as designed. In other
          words, the horse needs *free choice* grass forage 24/7.

     c.   Live within a herd. For safety, not for fun. There
          is safety in numbers. Separation from the herd
          creates emotional stress, and emotional stress at-
          tacks the physical body, and bad things happen.

     d.   Have the dietary choices available to them to keep
          themselves healthy and strong. A horse's genetics

know what the horse needs and when. For example – when a horse needs a liver cleansing the
brain will send him after thistle. When he needs
vitamin E it might send him searching for a
blackberry. Etc. If he's eaten quite enough of
high-sugar grasses, the hypothesis is he'll switch to
the low sugar grasses to balance. When humans
attempt to perform these functions, it's usually
pure guesswork, and usually late.

I sat on the porch and pondered these for a while. Clearly the
more the domestic horse could live and eat like his wild counterpart
the healthier and happier he would be. We had a pretty good start
at this in California with our "Paddock Paradise" arrangement.
They were never confined, out 24/7 with the herd, and getting
plenty of movement, defined by placing their hay in more than 100
small piles all the way around their 1½ acre hillside pasture. Not
what you would typically call a pasture. There was no grass. Just
dirt and rock... and dust!

But had we been able to add grass it would've been a micro-
cosm of how horses live in the wild.

Or would it?

At the time, I didn't know how or what horses eat in the wild.
I assumed that grass was grass. Off to Google, landing on safe-
grass.org and a study of *What Feral Horses Eat* by Kathryn Watts.

Ahhh. Now we're getting somewhere.

Her study and several others found on the internet were pretty
much the same, varying only by geographical availability. The con-
clusions were that wild horses eat mostly (80% or better) native and
naturalized grasses of various species plus orbs (flowering plants
and weeds), shrubs of various kinds, tree leaves and bark, and more.
In other words, they have lots and lots of choices and they use
them. Ms. Watts found that all the grasses in the wild contained

lower sugars than any cultivated pasture grasses she's tested. And *some* of the wild grasses contain *substantially* less sugar than domestic pasture grasses. Thus the hypothesis that the wild horse will balance his own sugar by eating both kinds of grass, along with those orbs, shrubs, tree leaves, etc.

She also points out, as does Pete Ramey, that grasses in the wild tend to be "bunchy" or "patchy", not in thick, tightly-woven carpets like so many domestic pastures. So the horse in the wild has to move more, cover more ground, to get the same amount of forage that a domestic pastured horse is getting. The wild horse is getting less grass per acre, thus less sugar per acre. And more movement which helps digestion and circulation. Plus he's balancing his intake by what his body is telling him he needs. And he has a wide range of choices of forages to accomplish this as he goes about his day.

I was beginning to carve away at the answer. Only it was obviously not *one* "answer," but a whole bunch of answers.

We all want this to be simple, but like so much of life, it just isn't. There is not one *big* difference between the domestic pasture and the wild horse meadow that can solve the sugar problem. There are a *lot* of differences, and each one is important.

Yet the bottom line is simple. Replicate the wild horse lifestyle and diet as closely as your situation permits and you will likely be good to go. And your horse will thank you.

After digging into this for a while now I think I've found "the bugs on the leaves," or rather they have become self-evident, and there are a bunch of them.

Ready?

Here we go:

First, most domestic horse pastures are:

1.   Only a single species of grass and nothing else. No orbs, or shrubs, or weeds, or trees. Nada. One choice for the horse. Eat it or go hungry.

2.   That single species of grass is usually a "cool season" grass like orchard or timothy because they grow longer into the cooler seasons. Cool season grasses are much higher in sugar content than "warm season" grasses because the cool season grasses contain fructan. Fructan that can continue to build forever as long as there's sun for photosynthesis. Warm season grass contains no fructan, only starch. Starch that is self-limiting because once the organ that holds it is full, production stops. Kathryn Watts has found cool season grasses to have NSC (sugar) percentages as high as 25+%. Warm season grasses are much, much less. The generally accepted NSC maximum as a percentage of a horse's overall diet should be 10% or less.

3.   That same single species of grass is usually a genetically modified species to make it heartier and grow longer into the cool seasons. Kathryn Watts' studies find that genetically modified and "improved" grasses are consistently higher in sugar than any natural or unmodified species.

4.   The single species of grass in a domestic pasture is usually heavily fertilized with chemical fertilizer (to make it even richer, and thicker). Chemical fertilizer contains large amounts of potassium which in times of stress can be feeding the horse levels of potassium a thousand times the amount he should be getting. This can cause all kinds of internal problems.

5.   The single species of grass in a domestic pasture is also probably sprayed with herbicides to kill every-

thing except the grass (plants and weeds that might be giving the horses some of the choices he needs). Note: Poison of any kind, regardless of manufacturers' claims, is not good for the delicate balance of the inner workings of the horse's gut.

6. The single species of grass is also probably sprayed with pesticides from time to time. Another poison.

7. And, lastly, the soil itself can be worn down and depleted of needed nutrients etc when planted and replanted with only the same seed every year, and fertilized and re-fertilized exactly the same year after year.

So I suppose if you're looking for one big issue to hang your hat on, it would be the issue of choice for the horse. Lots of choices. Not just one species of highly fertilized cool season grass. But rather many species of grasses, favoring low sugar warm season grasses like Bermuda, and lots of other stuff. All scatter-planted in patches and bunches. Not wall-to-wall. I cannot emphasize enough that if your horse has the choices he needs he will make the right choices to balance his diet and thus himself.

The perfect natural pasture for the horse will be ugly. Big time ugly. It will look uncared for. Not a nice, beautiful, thick carpet of a single species spreading out for acres.

On the following page are two photos of the wild horse meadow atop one of the Pryor Mountains of Montana where Cloud's band and many other wild horses hang out during the Spring and Summer. They head up as soon as the snow is melted and don't go down until they're forced to by the onslaught of winter weather. From a distance it looks for the world like any cultivated rich green pasture, but it's not even close. The horses have tons of choices to balance their own diets and apparently handle it all quite well.

Not your pristine, manicured pastoral scene you would expect to see driving through Kentucky, or even our little slice of middle Tennessee. As I said, wild horse pastures are ugly with a capital "U" but are just what the horse needs.

The following shots are a few looks at our hillside pasture, up close and personal. It's hard to discern in these small black-and-white photos, but each one contains at least some Bermuda, orchard, fescue, Dallis Grass and various orbs and un-named weeds.

As I write this in October, our herd's current delicacy is that flat seed of a weed that is covered in something like Velcro which sticks to anything that gets within yards of it. The horses come in with dozens of those awful things clumped in their forelocks, all over their faces, on their legs, everywhere! As I pull these pesky seeds off, if I also remove the hair that came off with them, the horses usually want to eat them out of my hand. Obviously there's something there they need or want. If a horse is getting plenty of what he needs or wants, he simply will not eat something that's bad for him. But if he's hungry and something bad is the only choice he has he will eat it.

How many acres per horse? The only answer I know is: *it depends.*
We're at approximately 3.5 acres per horse. Last fall, when we arrived, just after we had bush hogged maybe a third of it that had
been allowed to grow wild with virtually no grass, and before we
had sewn any seed, I was worried that the pasture wouldn't be large
enough. But after sewing quite a bit of orchard and Bermuda this
spring and summer, there's still plenty of grass in October. I think
we're going to be fine. For cutting we follow Melanie Bowles' philosophy at the Horses of Proud Spirit Sanctuary. Never shorter
than 4", never longer than 12".

Our two pastures are both open to all the horses at all times. When we moved in, neither pasture had been fertilized for at least eight years. Of course I didn't have sense enough to ask that question before we bought the property, but for reasons I have never really understood, once again God was taking care of us. The population was mostly weeds when we arrived but we found that once it had been bush hogged there was quite a bit of fescue, Johnson grass and Dallis grass underneath just begging for sunlight. You might recall that rain wasn't an issue last Fall. We planted maybe 50 pounds of Orchard at the tail end of the season. It was already too late for warm season Bermuda but I didn't know about the difference in sugar levels at that time anyway.

By Spring I was armed with research and when we started sewing the mix was heavily skewed toward Bermuda. Maybe a third of it was orchard grass. And, now, all of it seems to be doing very well.

We continued to feed one bale of hay a day during the hot season, split between morning and night, scattered over a long path through the pastures, just because we are still in transition and the added diversity as we attempt to build our "wild horse meadow" would help our own peace of mind if not our horses :). The enforced movement doesn't hurt either, although observation has confirmed that they'll make the trek from one end of the pastures to the other several times a day even without the hay.

So there it is. That's what we've learned and what we're doing. The logic of it all, as with so much of this journey, has left me wondering why in the world I didn't see it before. But in any case, our horses are the beneficiaries. To change over from a "traditional" pasture, I suspect, wouldn't be as difficult or take as long as one might think. And it's a whole lot easier to manage a mess than to keep a pasture pristine. Stop all chemicals. Throw out (by hand) a lot of differing seeds trying to favor warm season grass or at least

50/50 with cool season grasses. Hike into the nearest woods and bring back some weeds, seeds of weeds, and brambles, and shrubs. Take the fences off your trees. And manage the pasture only by cutting. Grass does well with cutting, weeds do not. So if you cut with Melanie's plan the weeds will not take over. They'll just be a presence. Or so I've been told, and it seems to be working for us.

And please remember, the object of all this is to be able to leave your horses out, living like horses, around the clock, 24/7, without worry about the amount of sugar your horse might be taking in. Or what that sugar might be doing to the health of your horses. To be able to let the horses monitor and manage their own diet and lifestyle instead of us micro managing their entire life. This is not to say that certain supplements might not be needed to cover deficiencies, which requires testing the grasses, perhaps the soil, observing the horses, and filling in the holes. But definitely cut out all processed feeds, all feeds with grain (sugar), and, of course, all sweet feeds. If you need added weight consider maybe a tiny bit of alfalfa, or rice bran (we use rice bran). Our small herd gets a small forage feed (Triple Crown Safe Starch) morning and night with rice bran and a few supplements top dressed, which I believe will be tapered off over time. But that is yet another topic. This one was all about what you can do to a sugar-unfriendly pasture to give your horses the lifestyle and health they were genetically designed to live, the lifestyle they deserve.

For their sake, please put the bugs back on the leaves.

Godspeed!

36

NOELLE HAS A SWEET SPOT

Unfortunately it was a tick bite, but at least it served a purpose. I could give her something she loved. A big, long scratch! This became the routine for more than a week, until the bite began to heal and was no longer itchy. I immediately looked around for another tick…nooo, just kidding. Anyway, around here you don't have to look far to find 'em in April.

I love it when Kathleen comes home, camera in hand. I tend to forget about these sweet moments until I start browsing through her weekend of photos. I didn't even know she was standing behind me when this next batch was taken. I had paused to play with Mouse for a moment. I'm always searching for easy things for her to do because that brain is always on, and always working. Easy for *me*, not her. She doesn't *need* easy. She gets everything so quickly.

She and Skeeter get their morning and evening Safe Starch forage (with our supplements added) in the side shed of the barn (see the Diet and Nutrition page on The Soul of a Horse website) They each receive a bit more than the other horses, Skeeter because he's older and Mouse because she's younger and still developing. The other horses would love to get to their feed so we lock the pair up to keep the others away. When I call Mouse out I usually try to play with her a bit before moving on. A couple of weeks ago I was gazing at Malachi's platform and thought *I wonder…* and Mouse and I began this little ritual.

I asked her to step up on the platform.

"Now walk on up, Mouse."
She's amazing.

"Now turn. Easy. Keep all your feet on the platform."
Which is not easy with those long gangly legs.

I was fascinated watching the wheels turn in that overactive brain of hers as she was figuring out how and where to place her feet so they wouldn't fall off the platform. One of her back hooves slipped off as she was rounding the corner and I said "Unh, unh, unhhh." And she immediately pulled it right back onto the platform and continued the turn. A couple of our horses would look down at that platform built for a baby and say *No thanks. I'll pass.* They probably wouldn't even try.

"Good girl."
She tucked in and made the turn
without losing another foot.

These photos were taken after a couple of weeks of working with her but the captions above are exactly how it happened on the very first day. I was quite simply amazed. *Now I walk a full 360 degrees around the platform very quickly and she stays with me without missing a beat. Malachi would be proud.*

One morning I was in a hurry. After she had stepped up, and walked all fours up, I gave her a quick rub and a treat and scurried off to open a gate. I heard a snort and when I looked back she had made the 180 degree turn all by herself and was just standing there looking at me.

Where are you going? We weren't finished.

I laughed out loud... and of course she got another rub and another treat. She's a special little girl. Well... no longer little I'm afraid. Except in age.

On the morning these photos were taken, while I was working with Mouse I didn't notice Cash mosey up. Kathleen did and snapped the photo below. "He was watching everything y'all were doing," she said. "Maybe he'll get up on the platform and do the whole routine for you."

When I saw the look on his face I had to laugh. I don't believe doing the routine is what he had in mind.

Who, me? Do that silly circus stuff? I don't think so.

Come back soon, my Sweetie. I miss you, and your picture taking, and I suspect of our readers do as well.

37

A ROUND PEN
FOR NOELLE

Finally. By mid-June we had enough days of dry weather sandwiched together to get the grading done *and* get the pea gravel delivered and *voila!* At last we have a round pen.

Kathleen returned for a month in early July - with her cameras - and our plan was to begin work with Noelle in earnest. No more excuses. A Join-Up and a lead rope were in her immediate future. Then summer hit suddenly.

With a vengeance.

Yet another record.

The hottest summer in middle Tennessee in thirty years.

We didn't get much done.

There was one period of twenty-plus days well over 100 de-grees, several of them into the hundred-and-teens. With humidity in the upper eighty to low ninety percent ranges.

We just couldn't get up for serious work outside.

And in early August Kathleen had to return to California.

A month *was* enough time to get used to living like we were supposed to be living. It was the first time in almost a year that we were able to spend that many consecutive days together.

And then she was gone.

No fair!

Meanwhile we did get Noelle to at least greet the round pen. We left two panels and two gates open so the horses could use it as a pass-through into the paddock in front of the barn where Noelle gets fed. The first morning Noelle cautiously strolled down the hill and into the pen through two open panels, sniffed around for quite some time, then walked toward the gate into the paddock, stopping cold a few feet away. The huffing and puffing began. This is one scary gate, only six feet wide, surely designed especially to eat mus-tangs. But there was her feed tub, not far away on the other side of the gate. She thought and huffed and thought and puffed... and finally bolted through the gate at a dead run. *Whew!* It was good to know that mustang mares are faster than round pen gates. But, af-ter mealtime, without that good Safe Starch forage as an incentive, it was a no go. She got really close to the gate at one point and some part of it scared her so bad she did a perfect rollback, front feet all the way off the ground for the full 180, before racing off across the paddock. I think it might've been the metal cross piece on the ground at the bottom of the gate, but I was up in the pasture scattering hay by then and couldn't tell for sure. She ultimately dis-covered that the back end of the barn breezeway was open to the pasture so off she went.

After several days of the same, never going out to the smaller pasture through the round pen, I ultimately closed all paddock gates except the one into the round pen and began a ritual of "pushing" her by walking behind her – *well* behind her – toward the round pen gate. She'd get too close for comfort and race off circling around behind me… and we would begin again.

Finally she got the idea. I wasn't going to go away until she went through the round pen gate. After six or seven tries, she finally backed off about thirty feet and ran at full gallop up the little hill and through the gate, not even slowing down until she had cleared the round pen completely and was out in the pasture.

It took several more episodes like this before she would walk through the gate into or out of the round pen relatively calmly. And finally she reached a point where it's no big deal going either way. Or stopping inside the pen to munch some hay out of the back of the gator.

One cooler day, relatively speaking, I took Mouse and Cash and the big red circus ball into the round pen and we all had a blast. Cash and I played pitch and catch like we used to in California. He hadn't forgotten a thing, as if it were only yesterday. Mouse 's first reaction was curious fear. She'd reach out and touch it, and jump back like a jack rabbit. But very soon she was interrupting Cash and my game so she could push it herself. She and I will have some fun if it ever cools off.

When Kathleen came back for a few days in late August she took her big ol' Palomino sofa Skeeter into the round pen a couple of times and worked him from the ground, then rode bareback with just a halter, trying to bring back the muscle memory. Neither of us had ridden in almost a year.

The photo below is one of those near-perfect days that allowed things to dry out enough to get the work done for the round pen. The skies were clear, the pastures had just been bush hogged, and everything was just gorgeous. I'm sure someone is going to screech *Did you say pea gravel in the round pen?! Are you nuts?* The answer to both, of course, is *yes*. But pea gravel is, in fact, terrific for bare hooves. Especially in this ground soaked climate. It does a bit of rasping and stimulates the soles and the frogs, promoting good blood circulation. We put a base down of crushed limestone (called crusher run) so the pea gravel wouldn't sink into oblivion.

Some of the boys and girls had some plant allergy issues through the Spring and Summer and the cumulative opinion seems to be that it'll take up to a couple of years for their immune systems to become adjusted to all the flora they've never encountered before. But their feet came through the wettest fall, worst winter, and most flooded spring ever in excellent shape. All except Noelle's. But we made the decision way back that we wouldn't let her hooves get in the way of allowing relationship to evolve at its own pace. I haven't known many mustangs but she is definitely the freakiest. And I think her feet have grown tired of waiting for her brain. So she began trimming herself.

Believe it or not, when I saw this flap I wasn't terribly worried. On that same morning Kathleen found this clump of mud that that had dropped out of one of her front feet beautifully in tact.

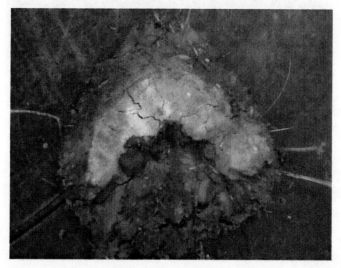

Note how the live sole area is almost perfectly defined in white (exfoliating powdery sole material I presume) as is the ridge between the live sole and the lamellar wedge that Pete Ramey talks about so often in his DVD set. Everything forward of that ridge is lamellar wedge (no vascular system… pretty much worthless material – stuff that the natural hoof specialist or the horse itself will ultimately do away with). As part of studies of the Australian wild Brumby by the University of Queensland, they captured a mare in a herd located in a climate similar to ours here in middle Tennessee and introduced her to a stallion in a herd in the desert. When she was released to the herd in the desert her feet looked pretty much like Noelle's. When she was recaptured three months later (she wore a GPS collar) her feet were perfect. Beautiful. In just three months! Which comes from traversing the kind of terrain her genetics evolved in for millions of years.

The next day that flap on her right front broke off, very cleanly. I wished I could put a mustang roll on it.

A couple of days later the other side broke off. Sorry for the soft focus on the two photos below. It was cloudy dark that morning when I shot them with my cell phone. I was watching the situation closely and if anything scary were to happen we would've done what needed to be done. But I thought then she was just trying to take care of what she wouldn't yet let us take care for her… yet.

Later that morning, the last flap had broken off.

If I could've taken a rasp to that foot it would've looked as good as any in the herd. Good girl Noelle. Thanks for showing us how it's done.

38

WHAT ARE WE THINKING?

Less than five years ago we didn't have a horse or a clue. And now we're holding tele-conference workshops on horse care with folks from all over the world. Sometimes I just shake my head and think how completely arrogant!

Fortunately Kathleen and I seem to be on opposite flip-flops between feeling "less than" and knowing we are solid in the research we have uncovered, regardless of how many people with decades of equine experience tell us we're nuts.

Then there are the continuous flow of emails every week that tell us of more happy, healthy horses now barefoot... or another healthy horse no longer eating packaged sugar in his diet... or one that is no longer in a jail cell and is free to roam 24/7 with a herd. It makes my day every time I receive one of these. They definitely make the effort worthwhile.

The workshops are gathered under the banner of *A Crazy Little Thing Called Love,* for obvious reasons, and the two we've held as of this writing are: **Why Would You Ever Let Your Horse Go Barefoot?** - and – **Why Would You Ever Let Your Horses Eat That?**

Both were roughly two-and-a-half hours long with several of the top people in each field participating. The recordings are available for download by clicking the Tele-Workshop buttons scattered around the website and the blog. But I know how intimidating it feels to think about carving two-and-a-half hours out of a busy schedule to listen to a workshop. Yet the information is important so I've included the summaries of each workshop below. A list of links relating to each topic can be found in the Resources section at the end of this book.

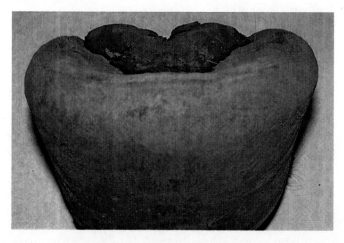

Pete and Ivy Ramey spent a couple of weeks camping in wild horse country out in The Great Basin of the western United States. While there, Pete stumbled upon a dead mustang who had broken a leg caught in a cattle guard (which parenthetically shouldn't even be there because it is illegal for cattle to be on the lands the 1971 Wild Horse Law designated to be principally for the wild horses). The photo above is one of the hooves from that mustang. It's like a piece of sculpture, and so sound and solid and strong that the horses were gliding effortlessly over terrain made up principally of lava rock so coarse that Pete said you could rasp a hoof with one of the stones.

Our first workshop is founded in the fact that the genetics of the wild horse and the domestic horse are exactly the same, as they've always been, evolved for millions of years, and unchanged for all the years horses have been under (so-called) domestic care. A domestic horse can grow a hoof every bit as beautiful, and strong, and sound as the photo above. Below are the summary notes from that workshop:

Summary Notes
Why Would You Ever Let Your Horses Go Barefoot?

Six Undeniable Truths:

1. **The first Undeniable Truth:** Science tells us that it would take a minimum of 5000 years - probably closer to 10,000 - to even begin to change the base genetics of any species. In other words, a few hundred years of selective breeding has no effect on base genetics whatsoever. Please log that in because this is the foundation for all that follows. Every-thing begins right here. The wild horse in the western high desert of the United States has incredible feet. He *must* have to escape predators and to travel the 10-30 miles a day he must travel in search for food and water. He's a flight animal. A prey animal. If he didn't have incredible feet he'd be extinct. We would have never known him. And the wild horse and the domestic horse of today are genetically exactly the same. Which means the domestic horse has the genetics to grow an incredible foot just like those in the wild. The domestic horse's foot is *not* geneti-cally weak and unhealthy. The conditions under which he has been living can certainly cause ill health, but the horse's genetics can fix that, given the opportunity.

2. **Undeniable Truth #2:** DNA sequencing was done on bones of horses discovered in the Alaskan permafrost dat-ing 12,000 to 28,000 years old… and that DNA sequenc-ing was compared to DNA sequencing from today's do-mestic horse… and there was less than 1.2% difference in those 28,000 year old horses and the horse in your back yard. Documented and on record. Confirming that the base genetics of every horse on the planet are the same. Science confirms for us that every horse on this earth "*re-tains the ability to return successfully to the wild or feral state*"

– note that the scientists say *successfully* – and that includes growing himself or herself a great foot that would protect this flight animal from predators and give him – or her – the ability to travel 10-30 miles every day of his life.

3. **Undeniable Truth #3:** The horse began and evolved for 50+ million years in and around the Great Basin of the western United States... then he crossed the Bering Straits Land Bridge into Siberia spreading into the rest of the world. Which means that the horse – as we know it today – spent 50+ million years evolving – now please get this because it's important – the horse spent 50+ million years evolving to live in conditions and on terrain like the western high desert of the United States. (See the DVD detailing Australia's University of Queensland research on the Wild Brumbies we discussed in the Workshop)

4. **Undeniable Truth #4:** Our horses will never adapt to the terrain and environment in our new home in middle Tennessee...or at least not for 5000 to 10,000 years... and it is therefore up to us – Kathleen and myself – to do everything within our power to replicate the lifestyle they would be living if they *were* living in the great basin – which is effectively the lifestyle they were living at our high desert home in southern California before moving to middle Tennessee.

5. **Undeniable Truth #5** (or perhaps #1): a horse's hoof is supposed to flex with every impact of the ground. Think toilet plunger. Every time it hits the ground it flexes outward – like a toilet plunger – and then snaps back when the hoof comes off the ground. That flexing sucks an enormous amount of blood into the hoof mechanism... keeps it healthy, helps it to grow properly, helps fight off problems... AND all that liquid provides an hydraulic-like

shock absorption for the joints, ligaments, and tendons of the leg. Wow... who knew. At one point I remember believing the horse's hoof just a wad of hard stuff... like one big fingernail. But there's more. When the foot lifts off the ground and the flexed hoof snaps back, the power of that contraction shoves the blood in the hoof capsule back up those long skinny legs, taking strain off the heart. So what happens to all this good stuff when a metal shoe is nailed to the hoof?

Nothing.

No circulation (or substantially reduced circulation)... no shock absorption (in fact if you've ever seen the videos of the vibrations set off up the leg when a metal shoe slams into the ground it'll freak you out)... and no assistance to the heart in getting that blood back up the leg. See the color thermograph on our website's barefoot page (www.thesoulofahorse.com/barefoot.htm). It's a study of the blood circulation of a horse wearing one metal shoe with the other three hooves barefoot. It's truly scary. I wonder how anyone can see this image and keep shoes on their horse. There is virtually no circulation at all in the leg and hoof with the shoe... and excellent circulation in the other three.

6. **Undeniable Truth #6:** There is no hoof lameness in the wild. Yet the American Farrier Association reports that more than 90% of *domestic* horses have some degree of hoof lameness? Some folks want to say that's because the domestic hoof is inherently weak. But as we've already established, the inherent genetics are the same as the wild horse. The reasons for so much domestic hoof lameness are

the metal shoes, diet, lifestyle, stress, and in some cases work load that we have forced upon the horse.

The ten questions to ask a farrier/trimmer before you hire him or her:

Are you exclusively barefoot? If not, this person does not truly believe in the history, the genetics, the science, and the facts. When we moved to Tennessee I never got past this question with several. Walked away. The best natural hoof professionals I know are passionate about being exclusively barefoot because they know a barefoot horse with proper diet and lifestyle will be healthier.

Do you exclusively follow the wild horse model? Unfortunately there are a lot of folks who claim to be Natural Hoofcare Professionals who do not have a clue (or the wrong clue) why it works or what the wild horse model is all about. Pass them by.

How important is diet and lifestyle to a successful barefoot experience? If they don't say (as Eddie, and Mark, and Pete Ramey, and so many others) that diet and lifestyle (movement) is as important as the trim, then walk away.

Do you incorporate the mustang roll? Eddie and Pete and Mark and others say this is the most important part of the trim. Must be used. Follow the wild horse example (photo above).

If the answers to the above are all positive, then continue:

May I have some references? Call clients of the hoof specialist and engage them in conversation. Get a sense.

Where did you get your training? There are no right answers here, but very important. Still it's a judgment call, combined with all the other answers.

How long have you been natural trimming? Important, but not the end-all. If only a short time it makes all the other answers even more important, especially the next two.

What sort of continuing education do you do? There is no right answer, but listen and be a good judge. If they say I don't really need any, walk away.

Who are your mentors or instructors you can go to when you need advice about a specific problem. Very important.

This last one is not a question per se but very important: If the person gets irritable or defiant because of these questions, or if you feel like the answers are BS, avoid this person like the plague.

Bottom line: You must find a trimmer who knows and understands how to help the horse grow the foot his genetics know how to grow, not someone who wants to "cut" the foot the way he thinks it should look... and it must be someone both you and your horse feel comfortable with. Seriously. Listen to your horse on this.

Genetic chronology of the horse:

Remains of the earliest animal anywhere in the world to bear recognizably horse-like anatomy were found in the Idaho-Utah-Wyoming area dating 52 million years ago.

Three-and-a-half million years ago the now famous fossils found near Hagerman, Idaho represent the oldest remains of the fully evolved genus Equus, roughly the size and weight of today's Arabian horse. At this time the horse had not yet migrated across the Bering Strait Bridge.

Bones found in North America and South America from horses that had migrated from North America dated one million years ago appear indistinguishable from Equus caballus (the modern day domestic horse).

DNA sequences taken from long bone remains of horses found preserved in the Alaskan permafrost deposits dated 12,000 to 28,000 years ago differ by less than 1.2% from modern counterparts.

The North America horse, along with sabre toothed tigers, mammoths, et al were apparently wiped out by an unknown cataclysm 7600-10,000 years ago.

The horse, Equus caballus, evolved exclusively in North America and crossed the Bering Strait bridge into Siberia and spread throughout the planet except for Australia and Antarctica (imported into Australia much later). Equus caballus was fully evolved on the North American continent and was migrating west well before the cataclysm of 10,000 years ago.

When the Spanish brought the horse to America in the early 16th century they were bringing him home. Back to his native land. Wearing the same genetics, the same DNA sequencing he was wearing when he left and when those left behind were wiped out.

The Summary Notes for the Workshop on Diet and Nutrition began with a list of Undeniable Truths similar to the Barefoot Workshop, plus additional ones relating specifically to diet and lifestyle. I've eliminated the duplicates in the list below to reduce the boredom factor :)... but they do still apply. Again, a list of links discussed during the workshop can be found in the Resources section at the end of the book. Dr. Juliet Getty, author of *Feed Your Horse Like a Horse*, was our special guest for this one. Returning from the first workshop were, of course, Kathleen and myself, Eddie Drabek (one of the premiere natural hoof care practioners in the U.S.), Scott Berry (who was one of three responsible for taking the entire Houston Mounted Police Patrol barefoot), and Mark Taylor (our natural hoof care professional here in Tennessee).

Summary Notes
Why Would You Ever Let Your Horses Eat That?

Undeniable Truths (Abridged):

1. **Undeniable Truth #5**: Movement is extremely important to a horse's lifestyle. They spent 50+ million years moving 10-30 miles a day searching for food, water, and staying away from predators. Every last snippet of their body depends upon that movement for good health, stress relief, digestion, blood circulation… and more.

2. **Undeniable Truth #6**: A horse in the wild will eat 16-18 hours a day… little bits at a time… mostly grasses. From the ground. For millions of years they evolved to do just that… so they have tiny little tummies NOT designed to eat 2 or 3 big meals a day… and their hind gut is expecting these little bits of grass forage virtually around the clock… and in fact actually needs it in order to function properly. And their physical structure is designed to eat from the ground. Bad things happen when they don't (see the video below).

3. **Undeniable Truth #7**: Horses ingest very, very little sugar in the wild. And when I say sugar I don't just mean raw sugar, candy or molasses. I mean anything that turns to sugar when it enters the body, which includes corn, oats – most grains actually – and of course molasses – even (are you ready) carrots. And grasses, some more than others. And remember your horse spent millions and millions of years evolving… without these sugars.

4. **Undeniable Truth #8**: Horses ingest NO hydrogenated oils or fats in the wild. Fats whose molecules have been mutated to make them more stable and give them a longer shelf life… and in the process play havoc inside a horse's body… or a human body for that matter. And virtually every packaged feed in existence is held together with either molasses or hydrogenated oils… or both.

Every time we deny these Undeniable Truths to our horses... every time we subvert the diet and lifestyle they were designed to live, we are doing them a massive disservice. Causing stress, encouraging problems ... and we are not giving them that crazy little thing called... love.

From Dr. Getty:

Feed Your Horse Like a Horse:

The foundation for all equine diets begins with free-choice grass hay and/or pasture, around the clock, 24/7.

Horses are meant to be "trickle feeders" -- eating small amounts of forage virtually all day long. This is due to their small stomach size in relation to the rest of their digestive tract, and the fact that their stomachs, unlike our own, produce acid continuously. Chewing produces saliva, a natural antacid, which prevents erosions (ulcers) from stomach acid.

• Horses need grass forage flowing through their digestive tracts at all times to prevent ulcers and colic, and maintain normal motility.

• The digestive tract is made of muscles and must be exercised through a constant, steady supply of forage.

• Excessive feeding of cereal grains leads to increased acid production, obesity, and insulin resistance. Wild horses do not develop these disorders. Cereal grains all have very high glycemic indexes, turning to sugar almost immediately once in the body.

• Cereal grains should only be fed, in moderation, to horses that have high performance/work demands. (Joe says *never*)

• Horses that are exercised with an empty stomach are likely to develop acid-related problems since the stomach secretes acid continuously.

• The hindgut bacteria are essential for a horse's well-being. Stress, high-starch diets, and antibiotics will diminish their numbers leading to ulcers, colic, and laminitis.

• Stress causes the production of cortisol (stress hormone), which leads to insulin resistance (elevated blood insulin).

• Elevated insulin = laminitis. A laminitic horse will experience relapses if placed in a stressful situation (e.g., forage restriction, isolation).

• Horses will self-regulate their forage intake when given the chance. Free-choice forage will allow for a horse's instincts in kick in, and he will eat only what his body needs to maintain a healthy weight.

• An overweight horse will remain overweight when stressed due to forage restriction. The key is to offer hay free-choice. Feed more, and the horse will eat more. Feed more than he wants, and he'll eat only what he needs.

• Once fresh grass is cut, dried, and stored as hay, it loses several nutrients including vitamin C, vitamin E, beta carotene (converted to vitamin A within the horse's body), vitamin D, and omega-3 fatty acids. Therefore, supplementation for hay-only diets is probably necessary.

• A horse who is stressed by "stall rest" will take a longer time to heal from an injury/illness.

Additional notes (more undeniable truths):

• You can prevent colic with proper diet and lifestyle

• Laminitis does not happen in the wild

• Ulcers are caused by human intervention

• An overweight horse will stay overweight if you restrict forage

• Horses experience stress and develop illness because of it

• An injury will take longer to heal when the horse is stalled

• Movement should be a constant in the horse's life

• Insulin resistance can be prevented, managed, and even reversed

More notes:

Horses need movement, movement, movement around the clock.

Horses in pasture need multiple choices of various grasses, even weeds, brambles, trees. Lots of choices. All unfertilized. Chemical fertilizers are terrible for horses. Causes ingestion of very high levels of potassium.

All sugars should be removed from a horse's diet. Sugar and feeds that turn to sugar. Especially grains, molasses and sweet feeds.

Feeds containing hydrogenated and heat processed fats should be removed from a horse's diet.

Horse owners should gather all of the knowledge they can, the facts and scientific truths, then apply that to their specific situations, horses, geographic locations, etc. There is no pat answer for all horses in all locations. Owners need to use knowledge-based judgment.

Horses have been designed over millions of years to eat from the ground, not from table-high feeders and troughs. All sorts of bad things are happening when a horse eats continuously from well above ground.

Oats have the second highest glycemic index of all unprocessed feeds, second only to corn (Corn 117, Oats 100).

The equine diet should be under 10% NSC (Non Structured Carbohydrates - which turn to sugar in the body) but most processed feeds run from 20% NSC to well above 40%. Purina only has two feeds out of 16 labels that are 10% NSC. All others are above.

Joe uses and recommends Triple Crown Safe Starch which is a forage in a bag. He calls it chopped salad. A chopped forage of orchard and timothy grasses guaranteed to be less than 10% NSC.

Once again, I highly recommend that you download the audio from both tele-workshops and play through them as you have time. They have tons of good information, all delivered in a very rich conversational setting. Therefore interesting, not preachy.

39

FEAR AND FAITH

Mariah Heals Herself

Sometimes it's hard to stay on the horse's end of the lead rope. To think about things from the horse's perspective. Whether it relates to training or lifestyle.

I'll never forget standing out in the rain one cold October day, soaked from head to foot because the rain wasn't expected. The temperature was only in the mid-fifties, but to me, sopping wet, that was freezing.

I looked at our horses, heads down, dripping with water, and I just couldn't stand it. I went for the halters and lead ropes and brought them into their covered stalls. The stalls were open, actually only half-covered, with one solid side facing the usual weather assault, but if we'd had a cozy barn with central heating and warm fuzzy pillows I'm sure I wouldn't have hesitated to take them right in. Or cover them with blankets had there been any available.

It's difficult for humans, especially when cold and wet, to understand that the horses do *not* feel like we do. Or eat like we do. Or react like we do. Or live like we do. We want to believe that the horse will always be better with human intervention. Human "help." How can they possibly make it without us?

Later that month I was wandering through a barn in northern Idaho. As I walked down the center aisle, I was struck by how clean it was. Pristine! When the owner happened by I said, "Do you never use this barn? It's so clean."

"Oh sure," he said. "We use it for hay storage."

"What about the horses?"

"They like to be outside."

"Even in the winter? In the snow?"

"Yep."

We were only twelve miles from the Canadian border. Winters are not warm here. I was amazed.

The owner walked around the barn to show me a lean-to he had built which was attached to the side of the structure. Just a roof, with divided stalls, to keep the horses separated when eating their supplements. They had free access to this shed, but never came into it except for the feed. Again, I was amazed. This ran so counter to everything I felt for my horses. We want to think of them as children, or big dogs, and treat them in the same manner.

They aren't children, or big dogs.

Not even close.

What sometimes seems too simple for me to grasp is the fact that horses have been around for all those millions of years, evolving to survive as a prey species, and those evolved genetics are precisely the same for every horse on the planet, wild or domestic. Given the opportunity they can take care of themselves. They're built to do it. If not, we would have never heard of the horse. They would've been extinct eons ago.

At both our former California home and the new one in middle Tennessee we have worked hard to mimic the wild horse lifestyle as closely as possible. But it never fails. Just when I think I've *got* it, when I'm certain I understand the concept...WHAP!

Along comes a blow to test my faith.

Mariah quite suddenly went dead lame in her right front foot. With a pounding digital pulse. Couldn't put any weight on it al all. An abscess! Apparently a bad one.

Fear rushed in and faith went right out the window.

It could've happened a few days earlier, before Kathleen and the twins returned to California to dig in for their last high school year. But it didn't. No, it had to be while I was home alone. With no one to help, or soothe, or listen. I was frozen in place.

Freaked out.

Tharn!

I love that word from *Watership Down*. It's rabbit-speak, and there is simply no English equivalent. It's what happens when a rabbit gets caught in the headlights and is so suddenly petrified that he can neither move nor think.

I was tharn. Our vast experience with horses – almost 5 years now – had never shown us an abscess. I was told gory stories of digging out all this gross-looking stuff with a knife and soaking the horse's hoof several times a day. High doses of antibiotics. And all the terrible things that can happen if it's not properly cared for. I was so tempted to violate my firm beliefs, my faith in Mariah's systems and the wild horse lifestyle, and lock her up because she was obviously in a great deal of pain trying to walk and keep up with the herd. But keep up she did, wherever they went. It was painful to watch. I was told the vet should come and dig it out.

I tried soaking her foot in Epsom salts. But she quickly grew tired and annoyed with keeping her foot in a tub for fifteen minutes at a time and finally she said *enough!*

And: *Where's my herd?!*

Determined, she found them, and with each step seemingly excruciating, she followed them off to the grove (she's last in the photo above). Deep down I of course knew that movement meant blood circulation and circulation meant healing but it was buried too deep for me to find and take comfort in at the moment. *But remember this please: stalling a horse with such a condition is exactly the wrong thing to do.*

Mariah followed the herd all the way to the grove on the far end of the western pasture, a quarter of a mile away from the first photo above. Here she is surrounded by the herd, all just out of frame. With a long walk back to the barn.

I had to quit watching her move. It hurt *me* too much.

"Get a soaking boot. You have to soak," someone said.

I made several phone calls and went out and bought a soaking boot.

It was never used.

When I arrived back at the house with the boot there was an email from Yvonne Welz, the amazing editor of *The Horse's Hoof*. She said: *Joe, when a horse has healthy hooves, abscesses are often here today, gone tomorrow! Just not a big deal. Yes, when the hoof has good blood circulation and lots of movement, the body just absorbs the problem area. Why do abscesses happen in healthy horses? Some sort of trauma or environmental cause, usually.*

Natalie Cruz of Shoe Free Performance Horses went a step further: *The vets won't like this but abscesses will heal themselves. The best thing you can do for your horse is give it a couple of tablets of bute a day for a week or so and baby the horse a bit for your own peace of mind. Keep the horse turned out so it can move which increases blood flow so the abscess either blows out or disintegrates inside the hoof. But check to make sure the horse was not kicked or otherwise injured, of course. If not, and the horse is suddenly dead lame on one hoof, it is usually an abscess. Take a couple of aspirin for your own headache and wait it out. But don't allow anyone to dig it out! This is counterproductive to healing and can actually introduce bacteria into the hoof and cause problems! No need to wrap the hoof either. It just annoys the horse and doesn't help its healing one iota. So drink a glass of wine and prop your own foot up instead. :) Some drawing products like Epsoms salt may help a little bit though I don't use any of them.*

I had barely finished reading these when suddenly Mariah was better. Limping, but putting weight on the hoof. The next morning she was walking fine. A day later she was cantering down our steep hill with the herd racing to the barn for breakfast.

A few months ago we had watched an abscess on Skeeter's belly (caused by an allergic reaction) slowly disappear as the body dissolved it. Likewise my tharn-ness began to dissolve away leaving an embarrassed logic. Of course, it's the blood circulation that does the dissolving. So why shouldn't Mariah's body do it's job. She has terrific circulation in her feet because she wears no shoes. She gets tons of movement which increases circulation even more. Her diet is good. And her body is working as it's designed to work.

The verse *Oh ye of little faith* came to mind.

Unfortunately appropriate.

The lesson? Nobody says it better than Rick Lamb: *Give them as natural a life as possible. Then get out of the way.*

Anybody want to buy fifteen pounds of Epson Salt?

40

TRUST YOURSELF TO TRY AND ERR

For years I've called the process of making Benji movies trial-and-error film making. I always – well, usually – know what I want to see up there on the screen, but almost never know how to get it on film. I remember late one night in Oregon on *Benji the Hunted* there were about twelve of us crammed and bundled around the camera which was sitting on the dirt pointed down at a tiny little cougar cub who was supposed to be looking up at Benji, pleading with his eyes to not be left alone to be eaten by some larger predator (his mama had been shot by a hunter). The look in the cub's eyes had to be right. It had to make us (the audience) choke up a little, feel the plight of this poor helpless baby. So there we were, this huge crowd of people all scrunched in a ball gawking down at this wee cub with a bevy of bright lights in his eyes, and I was supposed to be holding the "look" of the cub (as if he were gazing up at Benji) and I was also supposed to be doing something that would evoke just the right expression. Something that would make the cub's eyes beg pleeeze don't leave me here…

I squawked annoying sounds, tried to whistle (which I never had learned to do properly), gurgled, cracked sticks, rustled leaves, squeaked… none of which was having any effect. After a moment, the cub began to rock back and forth and I said, "I think he's falling asleep!" I got louder, but the little guy's eyes rolled back in his head and his eyelids dropped shut. He was out like a light. After a moment, he plopped over on his side, which woke him up with a start, and we began again. It had to be a funny sight to an innocent bystander. But it took a while for me to see the humor in it as rolls upon rolls of film raced through the camera. We shot up at least twenty minutes worth before finally getting the expression I wanted. I don't even remember what sound or movement extracted the perfect look… but that particular moment in the finished film is magical. Truly magical.

The point here is we don't have to know all there is to know every time we enter a new situation. We don't have to wait and wait until we're living experts of the moment to give something a try. I'm a huge advocate of book and DVD learning, of ingesting years of experience in a short time from people more knowledgeable than I. But there comes a time when there is no better learning than first-hand experience, of getting out there and trying something. Giving it a shot. Knowing full well that it probably won't work. But mentally set to keep going. To try something else. And something else again. Until that magical moment happens.

I've never forgotten the following moment, as described in *The Soul of a Horse*:

Our growing library of books and DVDs all said "begin at the beginning," which meant standing in the arena teaching my horse to back up, or move sideways. Or come to me. These exercises would give me control, said the DVDs. And once I had complete control over how, where, and when the horse moves, I would then have a safe horse. And only then should I climb aboard.

But I wanted to know why.

I was also anxious to take the next step with Cash. After Join-Up, he was now looking to me for leadership, so off we went to the arena.

I hear we learn by our mistakes.

One of the training DVDs had spelled out three different ways to teach backup.

See Cash back up, Method One.

See Cash back up, Method Two.

See Cash back up, Method Three.

Why, I wondered, did I need three? Especially here, beginning at the beginning. One method would've been quite enough to confuse both of us this first time out.

See Joe look like a circus clown.

Clumsy and awkward do not adequately describe the moment. I had Cash's lead rope in one hand and a three-foot-long Handy Stick in the other. A Handy Stick is a plastic rod used to extend the length of one's arm so that, hopefully, one can stand back far enough to avoid the kind of knockdown Kathleen got to experience. The stick, sold of course by one of the DVD trainers, is not to be used for discipline, only for guidance. According to this particular DVD, I was supposed to be doing one thing with the lead rope and another with the stick.

It was like trying to rub circles on your belly with one hand while patting your head with the other.

I felt like an idiot.

Those droll cocks of the head and quizzical looks from Cash were coming at me like machine-gun fire. I expected him to burst out laughing any minute. I was clearly not getting through.

But I didn't give up. I kept trying, but trying different things. If this doesn't work, try that. Or something else. And slowly, over time, I began to see that it really doesn't matter *what* you do, but rather how well you communicate what you'd like for your horse to do. If touching his ear will communicate that you want him to roll over, so be it. Ultimately I reached a point where I can now ask Cash to back up with nothing more than a look, or a toss of the head, or a flick of a finger.

And it all came about stumbling around through the process of trial and error. Which lead me to look at communication from his end of the lead rope, not from mine. I recommend it.

41

ARE YOU LIVING
YOUR PASSION?

Every time I look at one of these photos of Kathleen's and think about how much I lusted after the very life we're living I have no choice but to reflect upon how very blessed we are. Have always been. I'll never forget asking my dad when I was a junior in high school, "How am I supposed to go about choosing a career? Where do I start?" His response was profound, and not of the times, and for some reason that surprised me.

"Do what you would do if you didn't have to make any money at it whatsoever. Only then will you be passionate about your life and your work. Only then will you do your best job. Only then will you be happy."

Steven Covey has his seven habits of highly effective people. Andy Andrews has seven decisions. There are twelve keys to success. Thirty secrets. Eight principles. Five things you must know. Eight ways to the top. Six lessons for a happy life.

But I believe my dad had it right. There's really only one thing you need. And that one thing drives all the others.

That one thing is passion.

Where does it come from? Why does it work? How do you find it?

Libraries and book stores are full of attempts to analyze the passion-driven vision of successful people by breaking down what they did or didn't do into neatly compiled lists. But there is no power in those lists. Only information. Information that is historical in nature and no more applicable to all people and all circumstances than is taste in wine, preference of religion, or choice of spouse. But the magical results of living a life of passion are available to everyone of you regardless of goals, dreams, age, gender or education. Anything is possible when you care passionately about it. With passion, obstacles are just that. Mere obstacles. Something to power over, or dig under, or find some way around. Without passion those obstacles usually win.

A few years ago (more than a few actually) I wrote a song for one of our films that began: *Sittin' on the sidelines ain't what living's all about; Waitin' in the wings, just to see how it turns out…*

"You'll never be accused of that," Kathleen said earlier today, peering over my shoulder as I wrote this. "Not even close."

She's right, of course.

And what worked for me can work for you.

Step into your wildest dreams.

Live your passion.

I recommend it.

42

WHAT A YEAR!

Today marks the one-year anniversary of our southern California herd's arrival in middle Tennessee, and what a year it's been, moving from the photo above to the one below.

Quite a difference. Driven home by a year of record-setting weather.

On September 17th, one year ago, our horses arrived, after dark, amidst seven inches of rain that went on to become 26 inches over the next four weeks. We were worried sick about their feet which were accustomed to the kind of terrain that horses are genetically designed to live in, like the Great Basin where they evolved for millions of years. Hard and rocky. Not at all unlike their California home. We had no idea that we were moving into the wettest fall on record in middle Tennessee and our horses would not even see dry ground for months, never mind hard and rocky. This would be followed by the worst winter in 25 years, the floodingest spring ever, the hottest summer on record, and as I write this the driest Fall in thirty years.

We had been warned over and over again that the herd life style would have to change, that horses cannot be out 24/7 on the rich sugary grasses of middle Tennessee. But we were determined to trust ourselves to figure it out. Determined that our herd would continue to live as natural a lifestyle as possible. And two of the most important elements of a natural lifestyle are lots and lots of movement... and lots of dietary choices that are as natural as possible. Which means many kinds of <u>unfertilized</u> grasses... and weeds... and brambles... and trees. Their new home met both criteria. The pastures had not been fertilized for at least eight years and contained a broad variety of "stuff." And with the water pond on one end and the best grazing on the far other end they would surely get plenty of movement. If they didn't we also knew how to force it with a bit of their favorite hay. The concept here is that horses in the wild do a spectacular job of taking care of themselves come what may, and as I continually point out, our guys and gals are genetically identical to horses in the wild. It's difficult sometimes to turn loose, to, as Rick Lamb says, "set 'em up for success then get the heck outta the way." But that's exactly what we did.

Almost all of the time. Well, *most* of the time. Okay, *almost* most of the time.

Even with all the records falling there were the good moments. The happy moments. The times when we actually stopped and soaked up the beautiful setting we had landed in. And we enjoyed.

The horses agreed. On the morning after they arrived we opened the paddock gate and let everyone except our mustang Noelle into the pasture for the first time. And they hit the gate running! It's been a while since I've seen such sheer joy. They ran and kicked and frolicked all the way to the far end of the smaller pasture and all the way back, then back again. They were free. I suspect in more space than any of them had ever been in before. Kathleen said "If this doesn't tell you how they're supposed to live I don't know what will." She was manning the video camera so we don't have stills of these moments but they were surely beautiful. Our herd was happy.

It became obvious, with the weather we were having, that the round pen was not going to get put up until spring and there would be very little progress with Noelle over the winter. So the day finally came when we felt it was time to let her join the herd. There were some pleasantries and some fisticuffs but within the first hour they were all grazing together and the herd had a new leader.

My fear was that Noelle would never come back in and our morning and evening feed-and-rub sessions would vanish. But that very night, at exactly the right time, she strolled back to her tub in the front paddock and whinnied. *Hello! Where's my dinner?*

The winter brought four snows and one freezing rain and we had to learn the hard way to keep horses away from the pond during a 22-day span of temperatures below freezing. Mariah skated out to the middle of the pond and fell through the ice. Fortunately it's only five feet deep and she managed thrash her way out. A house full of blankets and all the favored hay she could eat brought her through it none the worse for wear except for a slight scratch on her left rear.

Finally in late February we had our first four consecutive days of sunshine since the day we moved in. And spring began to push back all the chilling memories of winter.

Summer arrived and Cash and I began to ride again, the first times since fall, still barefoot and bitless. Kathleen even crawled on Skeeter in the round pen, *bareback*, barefoot, bitless, and with camera in hand, finally banishing the fear she had harbored for years.

Somewhere along the line we had read or watched a trainer say teach the horse to bend around your inside leg when making a turn. When I unlearned that I guess I failed to pass it along and Kathleen was still using the wrong leg on Skeeter. When she'd apply the left leg of course Skeeter would move to the right. Finally she figured it out on her own and once she started applying the correct leg Skeeter screamed *Yippee* and turned into a wonder horse. And the fear, bred from confusion, is now history!

Through it all and into Fall the horses have done super. The lessons learned and adopted about wild horse meadows have kept them moving and making all the right choices. Just this past week I've scene Cash slurping up a Morning Glory vine, Mariah pulling leaves off a tree and Mouse snuffling through the brambles along the fence. And, as mentioned earlier, they all seem to like those pesky weed seeds with the Velcro covering. Their feet, especially with all the nasty weather, even amazed our hoof pro Mark Taylor. Just a week before the anniversary, he proclaimed all feet in "great shape."

The above photo is Cash's front left after Mark's trim. "A picture perfect hoof," Mark said and asked Kathleen to come shoot it. Our vet, Dr. Bobby, came out and gave all the herd except Noelle a thorough checkup and everyone passed with flying colors. So here we are with six happy healthy horses, very well adjusted and loving their natural life… as we continue to receive our life lessons from each and every one. And we are replenished daily, hourly, by scenes like the ones above and below. That same evening Kathleen and I sat on the porch with a glass of wine watching the herd, and talking. "I know in my heart that the philosophy is correct," she said. "That our horses are living the life they should be living, and because of that they should be able to take care of themselves." She paused for a moment, then added, "But it surely feels good to see this first year come to an end and be able to see the hard cold proof of it all." I smiled, teared up a bit, and said simply, "Thank you God."

From our front porch.

43

IN REFLECTION

This book is truly the continuation of our learning journey so please forgive as I "lift" a few words from the Synthesis of *The Soul of a Horse* as I see no way to improve on them, and no reason to change the thrust of this journey.

Discovering the mysteries of the horse is a never-ending journey, but the rewards are an elixir. The soul prospers from sharing, caring, relating, and fulfilling. Nothing can make you feel better than doing something good for another being. Not cars. Not houses. Not facelifts. Not blue ribbons or trophies. And there is nothing more important in life than love. Not money. Not status. Not winning.

Try it and you will understand what I mean. Apply it to your horses, and your life. It is the synthesis of both this book and *The Soul of a Horse* and why each came into being.

There are many who teach relationship, riding, and training with principles of natural horsemanship. Others support the benefits of going barefoot with the wild horse trim. Still others write that your horse should eat from the ground, and live without clothes and coverings. Some promote day and night turnout, where your horses can move around continuously. I've found none who advocate the essentials of a wild horse meadow in their pastures. And few have explored how dramatically one without the other can affect the horse and his wellbeing. Few have put it all together into a single philosophy, a unified voice, a complete lifestyle change for the domesticated horse. When I gave Cash the choice of choice and he chose me, he left me with no alternative. No longer could it be what I wanted, but rather what he needed. What fifty-five million years of genetics demanded for his long, healthy, and happy life.

I'm still astonished when I think where Kathleen and I began such a short time ago, and where most horse owners still are today, training with dominance and cruelty, cooping up their horses in small spaces, weakening their natural immune systems, feeding them unnaturally, creating unhealthy hooves and bodies with metal shoes. All because most folks actually believe it's the right thing to do.

I believe that most horse owners today care about their horses and are operating, as we once were, with little more than emotional logic, old wives' tales, and very little real knowledge. I hope these books will be a crack in the armor, a small breeze if not the strong winds of change, a resource and stimulus for what needs to be done.

And a longer, happier, healthier life for all horses.

BORN TO BE WILD
THE SOUL OF A MUSTANG

Riding the Winds of Change

Joe Camp

1

The Herd

The golden stallion was pacing nervously. Something did not feel right. The matriarch of the herd felt it as well. They were both sniffing the breeze and scanning the horizon. There was nothing alarming in sight, just a sense. A sense developed over millions of years to assure survival for a prey species with no defenses whatsoever but to run. To take flight. It worked well or this herd wouldn't be here today. They would've been gone, extinct, thousands if not millions of years ago.

The stallion watched the wise old matriarch move around the herd waking those who were dozing and nudging those munching stubbles of grass. Telling all that they would be leaving soon. She was still fit, but getting on in age and slowing down. She would have to step down before long. The matriarch is the true leader of the herd, usually the wisest and most trusted mare. The one who decides when to move and when to stay. Where to eat and drink. When to sleep. The stallion is the protector. And the father.

There was a moment when the matriarch paused nose-to-nose with a young buckskin mare and they sniffed, and blew a greeting. Perhaps more. There was a special connection between these two. The buckskin was only six years old but seemed much older and wiser. The stallion had often watched her move through the herd, getting her way with little more than a look or a nudge. She was very confident and very curious, and had a funny little twist of her head whenever the stallion would do something she didn't understand. It reminded the big palomino of a special colt from long ago. His and the matriarch's. Maybe the matriarch had seen this as well.

Neither the stallion nor the matriarch knew why they were uneasy but they were and that meant *move on*. Predators are everywhere, often stalking the herd, waiting for an opportunity to isolate a young foal, or an old or sick member of the herd. They were always around. Cougars, wolves… and recently man… and machines.

The matriarch knew where she would lead the herd. Many needed sleep. And her instinct told her they needed cover. There was only one stand of trees within reach, along the bank of a stream so the herd could drink as well.

She gazed at the big stallion for a long moment, then turned to leave. The herd followed, with no questions asked, and with no knowledge of the changes that were on the horizon.

2

A God Thing

It was all Cash's fault.

This sudden loss of my sanity and my life being in danger.

But how can you not love Cash?

The day he came into my life he swept me off my feet. He was on the cover of my last book and probably the reason it's the only one I've ever had on a best seller list. One look into those big brown eyes and you're done. Toast. Everybody says so.

Yet all of this was clearly his fault.

Just a few short months ago had anyone suggested that we adopt a wild mustang I would've asked what the lunatic was smoking. We had a whopping total of three years experience with horses, none of them wild.

Wild as in horses who have never touched or willingly been touched by any human.

If such a suggestion had occurred my response would've been easy.

No.

As in *not now, not ever.*

God obviously knew this. And if you harbor the concept that God plays fair forget it.

He recruited Cash. The nicest, sweetest, brightest, most polite, gentlemanly horse I'd ever met. The horse who not only taught us how to have meaningful relationships with horses but with people as well. The huge guy on four legs who taught us more about leadership, patience, and persistence than any two-legged ever had. The dear friend who quite simply changed my life when he said to me of his own free choice, *I trust you.*

It all began with an odd phone call that sounded very much like a joke.

There was a family herd of thirty horses from an expensive bloodline that the caller wanted us to adopt. Immediately. All thirty of them.

I could only hear Kathleen's side of the conversation but her face told me something very weird was going on.

"No, I'm sorry. I don't care how valuable they are. We have no place to keep thirty horses. Nor could we afford to feed them."

There was a pause, then, "No we are not a non-profit."

"Are too," I whispered. That wasn't the intention of course. It's just the way it is in the horse world.

"Who told you that?" Kathleen asked into the phone.

I found out later that the caller had somehow made contact with a friend of Kathleen's mother who had told him that we knew everyone there was to know in the horse world. He should call us.

"Well Suzie is misinformed," Kathleen said.

Actually we did have a small network of friends with horsey ties, generated by emails and letters after publication of *The Soul of a Horse*. But Kathleen was convinced this guy was a kook. Who calls a complete stranger and offers her an entire herd of supposedly expensive horses, free for the taking, and wants it to happen now?

"No, really, I don't think we can help you," Kathleen said.

He asked her to write down his phone number. Finally she did, along with his name. And she hung up.

The man was looking for a tax write-off in exchange for giving the horses to a non-profit. The horses belonged to his wife who was now an invalid and could no longer care for them. They were being neglected because the man knew nothing whatsoever about horses. And he needed to move his wife to a place where she could get treatment.

"What kind of horses?" I asked.

"Polish Arabians."

The words caught in my throat. I tried to speak but couldn't.

"Polish Arabians?" I mouthed silently.

Kathleen's brow crinkled up in a knot.

"Am I missing something?"

"Cash is Polish Arabian," I squeaked. "Or is supposed to have Polish Arabian blood."

"And?"

"This guy is giving away thirty Cashes?"

"I don't think it works like that."

Kathleen was certain it all had to be some sort of scam. But I couldn't turn it loose.

Were all Polish Arabians of Cash's mindset, his personality? I was seriously bothered by the fact that thirty Cashes were being neglected. What if it wasn't a scam? What if the lives of these thirty horses were at stake?

"The man said there are twenty mares, most of them pregnant," Kathleen said, "and if he can't get a tax write-off he's going to sell them all at auction."

"What?!"

Selling at auction – not the high end fancy ones, the one's down at the local feedlots and fairgrounds – is usually for horses that can't be sold anywhere else and all too often this means a trip to slaughter houses in Mexico and Canada.

I went straight to the computer and sent an email with details and the man's phone number to everyone I knew who had any connection to horse rescue. Karen Everhart of Rainbow Meadows Rescue Sanctuary responded and said if the man would give her control over the herd she would see that they were all adopted out to good homes and she would run the adoptions through Rainbow Meadows so the man could get his tax write-off.

"Fantastic!" I said. "Wonderful."

Then a notion struck me.

I turned to Kathleen. "What would you think about adopting one of the pregnant mares?"

"We don't need another horse."

"I know."

"We can't afford another horse."

"I know."

"Much less two."

"I know. So what do you think?"

"I think I'm really angry at you," she said.

We're both beyond help. Even when we're late for an appointment, we'll pull over to the side of a road to watch a couple of foals romping in a pasture. We had talked about having a baby since the day we acquired our first mare. But fear of what could go wrong and our inexperience always talked us out of it.

But another Cash?

"Two Cashes," Kathleen grumbled.

"It would be a new learning experience."

"I know, I know," she sighed. "One that we know nothing about. One that we're afraid of. Yes I see where you're going. An interesting journey for the next book."

"Saving a mom and her foal from possible slaughter would be getting another good message out there."

"A whole raft of messages," Kathleen added. "Like why does anyone have thirty horses that they cannot afford to care for?"

I told Karen we'd take a pregnant mare.

Kathleen and I talked about it day and night.

"I wonder how far along she'll be?"

"How long is gestation?"

"I don't know"

"Me either."

Off to Google. And Amazon.

What a mistake that was. The first book to come in was 279 pages long and only a few of those pages were devoted to how things were supposed to work. The rest of the book went into graphic detail about all the things that *could, might, shouldn't* go wrong, and explained in some language other than English exactly what we were supposed to do about each one. The first instruction was to commit each symptom to memory along with precisely what to do should it occur.

I didn't get past the second chapter.

"Maybe we should rethink this," Kathleen said.

Our vet, Dr. Matt, assured me that 97% percent of all foalings were perfectly normal and should there be a problem he was not far away.

Kathleen began a list of all the things we were supposed to have on hand just for a normal foaling, then added the emergency stuff. The list would eventually grow to several pages.

I began to worry about how we would get the mare down to our place.

The herd was in northern California. We were in southern California. And I was, at best, still very inexperienced with our 25 foot horse trailer. Most trips were to the local park where we trail ride, just a few miles away. I had almost no hours logged on freeways, and the longest trip I had ever taken was barely over a hundred miles right through the middle of Los Angeles traffic. I was a wreck. Do I make mountains out of molehills?

Absolutely, Kathleen would say.

Dr. Matt said a mare shouldn't travel during her last thirty days of pregnancy. Which meant that a vet up there would need to look at our choice, confirm pregnancy, and estimate delivery time. But the mare was not the only one who needed more than thirty days. We didn't have a clue about any of this and needed time to study.

We began to make preparations to fly up, meet the herd, and make a selection.

And I was dreaming about the baby to come.

It was always the same dream. I awoke one morning and wrote it all down. The birth of our new baby.

"It's beautiful," Kathleen said. Her eyes were moist. "I hope that's the way it happens. It's very sweet and should be in the book."

But the concept for a book and the recurring dream all vanished quite suddenly one morning.

Poof.

Gone.

The horse owner's husband told us that someone had volunteered to adopt the entire herd and keep them together as a family.

"How fantastic is that?" I said when I told Kathleen about the call.

"You don't sound very sincere," she said.

"Of course I am. If it's for real what could be better for the horses?"

"Right," she said, sounding no more sincere than I did.

The truth was we were both stunned. In our hearts we were happy for the herd. But we couldn't help missing that mom and baby we felt like we already knew and loved.

The baby I had seen born over and over again in my dreams. The baby I had already written about. The passage Kathleen had said should be in the book.

It is, by the way.

It's the Preface you read back at the beginning. The piece that's pure fiction. Just a dream. But clearly it served its purpose for I was now in the soup so to speak. I actually *wanted* that endangered pregnant mare. The concept was no longer a foreign thought. I was emotionally invested. The sanity line had been crossed. I had already written about it. And now I was desperate to see how it would all work out.

"It's Cash's fault," Kathleen chirped. "You got sucked in because of Cash."

It's true. If the herd had not been Polish Arabian none of this would've happened. I would've tried to find someone who could help the horses and that would've been that.

Someone other than me.

"Living proof," I said.

"Of what?"

"God doesn't play fair."

"Would you play fair if you had to deal with you?"

I glanced over to see if she was smiling.

I couldn't tell.

Our friend Cate Crismani had been following the story so I called her to pass along the herd's gain and our loss. She was strangely ecstatic.

"I love it," she blurted. "Now you can adopt a pregnant mustang instead."

"Excuse me," I said.

Cate publishes *True Cowboy* magazine which devotes many of its pages to the plight of the American mustang.

"A piece of our national heritage is at stake," she went on. "The Bureau of Land Management has over 33,000 gathered mustangs in holding pens around the country and now they're all under a death threat from the U.S. Government Accountability Office."

"Mustangs are wild," I said.

"You can handle it. And you can make a huge difference for a national icon. You need to do this."

"I don't think so," I mumbled. "Two new Cashes I could handle. Two wild mustangs are indeed something else."

"Do it. You won't be sorry."

I hung up with my head spinning.

I had studied the wild horse lifestyle for the last book. But I knew very little about the issues surrounding the federal government's management of the species. Or why they were involved at all. Much less why they had 33,000 captured mustangs in holding pens around the country.

Back to Google.

It seems that most of the federal land allocated to the protection of wild horses in a 1971 law was subsequently leased to Ranchers to graze cattle and sheep. In violation of the 1971 law. The cattle and sheep were consuming the grass and water, leaving very little for the horses. So instead of removing the cattle and sheep, the federal government was reducing the wild horse herd sizes.

That made no sense. Surely I was missing something.

I found the 1971 law and read it.

I almost wish I hadn't.

The law clearly states that the land where these horses were living at the time (approximately 52 million acres of federal land) was to be *devoted principally* to wild free-roaming horses and burros. That means the wild horses and burros were to be the principal presence on that land. Not the exclusive presence but definitely the principal presence.

And on that land – *their* land by law – and *our* land, we the taxpayers - the horses and burros were outnumbered by cattle and sheep 150 to 1.

With a heavy sigh I pushed away from the computer and slumped back into my squeaky chair. Why me? I wondered.

That night after dinner I dumped it all on Kathleen.

There was a long silence.

"Do you think this is smart?" she finally asked.

"Probably not."

"Are you up to the task?" she asked.

I had watched the likes of Monty Roberts and Pat Parelli do incredible work with mustangs but they each had thirty to forty times my experience with horses. Horses of every imaginable kind.

"I don't know," I answered. "I really don't know. But it could be important to try."

"It's definitely not going to be like training Cash."

"Copy that," I said.

"Then it'll be your Christmas present."

Our original entry into the horse world began with Kathleen giving me a trail ride for my birthday. Two weeks later we owned three horses. Now a pregnant mustang for Christmas. What, I wondered, might Fathers Day bring?

3

The Machine

The roar was deafening. And very close.

Too close.

The matriarch fought her instinct to run. It was an ancient instinct developed over millions of years to keep her safe. And to keep the herd safe. But this time the matriarch knew that safety depended upon the cover of the trees. It was a foreign emotion to walk slowly among the herd, impassively, trying to keep them calm and together. But she had felt this pulsing thunder before, and had seen it. She knew what it was. So did the stallion.

The big palomino was searching the tops of the trees, trying to find the sound through the patchwork of limbs and leaves. It was getting louder. Closer. Every fiber in his body wanted to *run* but he remembered the last time. He remembered what could happen out in the open.

Suddenly there it was, right above them. Barely above the treetops. Whirling blades tearing at the tree limbs. There was much snorting and shuffling of feet but the matriarch and the stallion worked hard at keeping their own adrenaline at bay which helped the others.

The stallion had watched from high atop a rocky plateau as a machine like this had gotten behind another band from their herd and had driven them into a canyon surrounded by cliffs. Men appeared at the entrance and slammed metal walls blocking any escape. The stallion never saw any of this band again. The images racing through his memory were all filled with fear. Glassy eyes. Screams of anguish.

As the machine whirled off toward the setting sun the matriarch was already gathering her charges and moving them out of the trees in the opposite direction. The buckskin mare joined her at the head of the herd and broke their trot into a full gallop trying to put as much distance between them and the deafening noise as possible. She too knew what it could mean. Too well. The stallion brought up the rear. They ran, and ran, and ran.

It would be night soon and they would be safe. The matriarch was tiring but she kept pushing until she could run no more. Then she slept deeply, surrounded by her herd. The buckskin mare stood watch, the sentinel, scanning the distant horizons.

There was no sign of the machine. But the big golden stallion was still uneasy.

Nothing seemed to feel right anymore.

BORN TO BE WILD
THE SOUL OF A MUSTANG

Riding the Winds of Change

Publishing Date: Late 2011

RESOURCES

Valuable Links from the tele-workshop on Why Barefoot?

Kathleen and Joe's website:
http://www.thesoulofahorse.com

Kathleen and Joe's blog:
http://thesoulofahorse.com/blog

Eddie Drabek's website:
http://www.wholehorsetrim.com/

Pete Ramey's website:
http://www.hoofrehab.com

Excellent article on The Houston Mounted Police Patrol by Scott
Berry: http://www.liberatedhorsemanship.com/
Scroll down to the fifth Article in the column on the right entitled
Barefoot Police Horses

An article about the Houston Mounted Patrol on our website:
http://www.thesoulofahorse.com/HoustonPatrolStory.htm

To read about, sample, and order the DVD about Australia's University of Queensland study of the wild Brumbies in Australia:
http://www.wildhorseresearch.com/Documents/dvd%20order%20form.htm

Auburn University Vet School studies on healing with barefoot:
Dr. Debra (Ruffin) Taylor is the PhD in charge of the Auburn
University Vet School's studies on healing laminitis and navicular
problems via barefoot. Dr. Taylor's email is: ruffidc@auburn.edu

Links promised in the workshop are:
http://www.hoofrehab.com/AuburnUvetschool.htm

http://easycareinc.typepad.com/from_the_horses_mouth/auburn-
university-research/

http://www.hoofrehab.com/NavStudy.html

www.thesoulofahorse.com/NewsletterArchive.htm#Auburn

The next are 2 links to short videos of a horse's hoof hitting the
ground. One is a shod hoof, one is barefoot. Watch the vibrations
roll up the leg from the shod hoof… then imagine that happening
every time any hoof hits the ground:

Shod hoof video:
http://www.youtube.com/watch?v=fql-xsofeg0

Unshod hoof video:
http://www.youtube.com/watch?v=_6yLEdr2EOM

If you would like to see an example of how the internal structures
of the hoof tear at the lamina when the horse is shod or when hoof
walls are too long (Peripheral Loading) and if you have a strong
stomach:
http://www.youtube.com/watch?v=ej1MNNz2mgI

Video: of Joe: Why Barefoot?
http://www.youtube.com/watch?v=V2ZofRxB1bU

Video of Joe: Why Our Horses Eat from the Ground
http://www.youtube.com/watch?v=g1Gxkpr1hPo

Find a recommended trimmer in your area:

The American Association of Natural Horse Care Practioners
www.aanhcp.net

The American Hoof Association
www.americanhoofassociation.org

Pacific Hoof Care Practitioners
www.pacifichoofcare.org

Liberated Horsemanship Practitioners
www.liberatedhorsemanship.com/

Valuable Links from the tele-workshop on Diet and Nutrition
I have not duplicated links found above from the Barefoot Work-shop

Dr. Juliette Getty's website: http://gettyequinenutrition.biz/

Dr. Getty's favorite feed/forage testing facility:
Equi-Analytical Labs: http://www.equi-analytical.com

For more about pretty much anything in this book
please visit one of these websites:

www.thesoulofahorse.com

http://thesoulofahorse.com/blog

www.14handspress.com

www.thesoulofahorseblogged.com

CPSIA information can be obtained at www.ICGtesting.com
Printed in the USA
LVOW11s0134040615

441050LV00001B/59/P